Cram101 Textbook Outlines to accompany:

Uppers, Downers, All Arounders : Physical and Mental Effects of Psychoactive Drugs

Darryl Inaba, 6th Edition

A Content Technologies Inc. publication (c) 2012.

Learning System

Cram101 Textbook Outlines is a learning system. The notes in this book are the highlights of your textbook, you will never have to highlight a book again.

How to use this book. Take this book to class, it is your notebook for the lecture. The notes and highlights on the left hand side of the pages follow the outline and order of the textbook. All you have to do is follow along while your instructor presents the lecture. Circle the items emphasized in class and add other important information on the right side. With Cram101 Textbook Outlines you'll spend less time writing and more time listening. Learning becomes more efficient.

Cram101.com Online

Increase your studying efficiency by using Cram101.com's practice tests and online reference material. It is the perfect complement to Cram101 Textbook Outlines. Use self-teaching matching tests or simulate in-class testing with comprehensive multiple choice tests, or simply use Cram's true and false tests for quick review. Cram101.com even allows you to enter your in-class notes for an integrated studying format combining the textbook notes with your class notes.

Visit **www.Cram101.com**, click Sign Up at the top of the screen, and enter **DK73DW16915** in the promo code box on the registration screen. Your access to www.Cram101.com is discounted by 50% because you have purchased this book. Sign up and stop highlighting textbooks forever.

Uppers, Downers, All Arounders : Physical and Mental Effects of Psychoactive Drugs
Darryl Inaba, 6th

CONTENTS

Chapter 1. PSYCHOACTIVE DRUGS: HISTORY & CLASSIFICATION

Hallucination	A hallucination, in the broadest sense of the word, is a perception in the absence of a stimulus. In a stricter sense, hallucinations are defined as perceptions in a conscious and awake state in the absence of external stimuli which have qualities of real perception, in that they are vivid, substantial, and located in external objective space. The latter definition distinguishes hallucinations from the related phenomena of dreaming, which does not involve wakefulness; illusion, which involves distorted or misinterpreted real perception; imagery, which does not mimic real perception and is under voluntary control; and pseudohallucination, which does not mimic real perception, but is not under voluntary control.
ALCOHOL	In chemistry, an alcohol is any organic compound in which a hydroxyl functional group (-OH) is bound to a carbon atom, usually connected to other carbon or hydrogen atoms. An important class are the simple acyclic alcohols, the general formula for which is $C_nH_{2n+1}OH$. Of those, ethanol (C_2H_5OH) is the type of alcohol found in alcoholic beverages, and in common speech the word alcohol refers specifically to ethanol.
BARBITURATE	Barbiturates are drugs that act as central nervous system depressants, and, by virtue of this, they produce a wide spectrum of effects, from mild sedation to total anesthesia. They are also effective as anxiolytics, as hypnotics, and as anticonvulsants. They have addiction potential, both physical and psychological. Barbiturates have now largely been replaced by benzodiazepines in routine medical practice - for example, in the treatment of anxiety and insomnia - mainly because benzodiazepines are significantly less dangerous in overdose. However, barbiturates are still used in general anesthesia, as well as for epilepsy. Barbiturates are derivatives of barbituric acid.
MDMA	MDMA - colloquially known as ecstasy, often abbreviated "E" or "X" - is an entactogenic drug of the phenethylamine and amphetamine class of drugs. MDMA can induce euphoria, a sense of intimacy with others, and diminished anxiety and depression. Many, particularly in the fields of psychology and cognitive therapy, have suggested MDMA might have therapeutic benefits and facilitate therapy sessions in certain individuals, a practice which it had formally been used for in the past.

Chapter 1. PSYCHOACTIVE DRUGS: HISTORY & CLASSIFICATION

Opium	Opium is the dried latex obtained from the opium poppy (Papaver somniferum). Opium contains up to 12% morphine, an alkaloid, which is frequently processed chemically to produce heroin for the illegal drug trade. The latex also includes codeine and non-narcotic alkaloids such as papaverine, thebaine and noscapine.
Psychoactive drug	A psychoactive drug, psychopharmaceutical, or psychotropic is a chemical substance that crosses the blood-brain barrier and acts primarily upon the central nervous system where it affects brain function, resulting in changes in perception, mood, consciousness, cognition, and behavior. These substances may be used recreationally, to purposefully alter one's consciousness, as entheogens, for ritual, spiritual, and/or shamanic purposes, as a tool for studying or augmenting the mind, or therapeutically as medication.
	Because psychoactive substances bring about subjective changes in consciousness and mood that the user may find pleasant (e.g. euphoria) or advantageous (e.g. increased alertness), many psychoactive substances are abused, that is, used excessively, despite the health risks or negative consequences.
Morpheus	Morpheus in Greek mythology is the god of dreams, leader of the Oneiroi. Morpheus has the ability to take any human form and appear in dreams. His true semblance is that of a winged daemon, imagery shared with many of his siblings.
Cannabis	Cannabis is a genus of flowering plants that includes three putative species, Cannabis sativa, Cannabis indica, and Cannabis ruderalis. These three taxa are indigenous to Central Asia, and South Asia. Cannabis has long been used for fibre (hemp), for seed and seed oils, for medicinal purposes, and as a recreational drug.
Cannabis indica	Cannabis indica is an annual plant in the Cannabaceae family. A putative species of the genus Cannabis, it is typically distinguished from Cannabis sativa.
Ginseng	Ginseng is any one of eleven distinct species of slow-growing perennial plants with fleshy roots, belonging to the Panax genus in the family Araliaceae. It grows in the Northern Hemisphere in eastern Asia (mostly northern China, Korea, and eastern Siberia), typically in cooler climates; Panax vietnamensis, discovered in Vietnam, is the southernmost ginseng found quinquefolius. Ginseng is characterized by the presence of ginsenosides.

DRUGS: HISTORY & CLASSIFICATION

Chapter 1. PSYCHOACTIVE DRUGS: HISTORY & CLASSIFICATION

COCAINE	Cocaine benzoylmethylecgonine (INN) is a crystalline tropane alkaloid that is obtained from the leaves of the coca plant. The name comes from "coca" in addition to the alkaloid suffix -ine, forming cocaine. It is a stimulant of the central nervous system, an appetite suppressant, and a topical anesthetic. Specifically, it is a serotonin-norepinephrine-dopamine reuptake inhibitor, which mediates functionality of these neurotransmitters as an exogenous catecholamine transporter ligand. Because of the way it affects the mesolimbic reward pathway, cocaine is addictive.
Anticholinergic	An anticholinergic agent is a substance that blocks the neurotransmitter acetylcholine in the central and the peripheral nervous system. An example of an anticholinergic is dicycloverine, and the classic example is atropine. Anticholinergics are administered to reduce the effects mediated by acetylcholine on acetylcholine receptors in neurons through competitive inhibition. Therefore, their effects are reversible.
Ketamine	Ketamine is a drug used in human and veterinary medicine. Its hydrochloride salt is sold as Ketanest, Ketaset, and Ketalar. Pharmacologically, ketamine is classified as an NMDA receptor antagonist.
Khat	Khat is a flowering plant native to tropical East Africa and the Arabian Peninsula. Khat contains the alkaloid called cathinone, an amphetamine-like stimulant which is said to cause excitement, loss of appetite, and euphoria. In 1980, the World Health Organization classified khat as a drug of abuse that can produce mild to moderate psychological dependence (less than tobacco or alcohol). The plant has been targeted by anti-drug organizations like the DEA. It is a controlled or illegal substance in many countries, but is legal for sale and production in many others.
Stimulant	Stimulants are psychoactive drugs which induce temporary improvements in either mental or physical function or both. Examples of these kinds of effects may include enhanced alertness, wakefulness, and locomotion, among others. Due to their effects typically having an "up" quality to them, stimulants are also occasionally referred to as "uppers".

Chapter 1. PSYCHOACTIVE DRUGS: HISTORY & CLASSIFICATION

Hormone	A hormone is a chemical released by a cell or a gland in one part of the body that sends out messages that affect cells in other parts of the organism. Only a small amount of hormone is required to alter cell metabolism. In essence, it is a chemical messenger that transports a signal from one cell to another. All multicellular organisms produce hormones; plant hormones are also called phytohormones. Hormones in animals are often transported in the blood. Cells respond to a hormone when they express a specific receptor for that hormone. The hormone binds to the receptor protein, resulting in the activation of a signal transduction mechanism that ultimately leads to cell type-specific responses.
Theriac	Theriaca was a medical concoction originally formulated by the Greeks in the 1st century AD and became popular throughout the ancient world as far away as China and India via the trading links of the Silk Route. It was an alexipharmic, or antidote, considered a universal panacea, for which it could serve as a synonym: in the 16th century Adam Lonicer wrote that garlic was the rustics' Theriac or Heal-All. The word theriac comes from the Greek term θηριακ? (theriake), the feminine of θηριακ?ς (theriakos), signifying "pertaining to animals", from θηρ?ον (therion), "wild animal, beast".
Morphine	Supplementary data for morphine. Structure and properties
Opioid	An opioid is a chemical that works by binding to opioid receptors, which are found principally in the central and peripheral nervous system and the gastrointestinal tract. The receptors in these organ systems mediate both the beneficial effects and the side effects of opioids. Opioids are among the world's oldest known drugs; the use of the opium poppy for its therapeutic benefits predates recorded history.

Chapter 1. PSYCHOACTIVE DRUGS: HISTORY & CLASSIFICATION

Naltrexone	Naltrexone is an opioid receptor antagonist used primarily in the management of alcohol dependence and opioid dependence. It is marketed in generic form as its hydrochloride salt, naltrexone hydrochloride, and marketed under the trade names Revia and Depade. In some countries including the United States, a once-monthly extended-release injectable formulation is marketed under the trade name Vivitrol. Also in the US, Methylnaltrexone Bromide, a closely related drug, is marketed as Relistor, for the treatment of opioid induced constipation.
Substance abuse	Substance abuse refers to a maladaptive pattern of use of a substance that is not considered dependent. The term "drug abuse" does not exclude dependency, but is otherwise used in a similar manner in nonmedical contexts. The terms have a huge range of definitions related to taking a psychoactive drug or performance enhancing drug for a non-therapeutic or non-medical effect.
Narcotic	The term narcotic originally referred medically to any psychoactive compound with sleep-inducing properties. In the United States of America it has since become associated with opioids, commonly morphine and heroin. The term is, today, imprecisely defined and typically has negative connotations.
Interaction	In medicine, most medications can be safely used with other medicines, but particular combinations of medicines need to be monitored for interactions, often by the pharmacist. Interactions between medications (drug interactions) fall generally into one of two main categories: 1. pharmacodynamic : Involving the actions of the two interacting drugs. 2. pharmacokinetic : Involving the absorption, distribution, metabolism, and excretion of one or both of the interacting drugs upon the other.
Depression	Depression, one of the most commonly diagnosed psychiatric disorders, is being diagnosed in increasing numbers in various segments of the population worldwide. Depression in the United States alone affects 17.6 million Americans each year or 1 in 6 people. Depressed patients are at increased risk of type 2 diabetes, cardiovascular disease and suicide. Within the next twenty years depression is expected to become the second leading cause of disability worldwide and the leading cause in high-income nations, including the United States. In approximately 75% of completed suicides the individuals had seen a physician within the prior year before their death, 45%-66% within the prior month. Approximately 33% - 41% of those who completed suicide had contact with mental health services in the prior year, 20% within the prior month.

Chapter 1. PSYCHOACTIVE DRUGS: HISTORY & CLASSIFICATION

Decongestant	A decongestant is a type of drug that is used to relieve nasal congestion. The vast majority of decongestants act via enhancing norepinephrine (noradrenaline) and epinephrine (adrenaline) or adrenergic activity by stimulating the α-adrenergic receptors. This induces vasoconstriction of the blood vessels in the nose, throat, and paranasal sinuses, which results in reduced inflammation (swelling) and mucus formation in these areas.
Designer drug	Designer drug is a term used to describe drugs which are created (or marketed, if they had already existed) to get around existing drug laws, usually by modifying the molecular structures of existing drugs to varying degrees, or less commonly by finding drugs with entirely different chemical structures that produce similar subjective effects to illegal recreational drugs.
	History
	United States
	1920s-1930s
	The term "designer drug" was first coined by law enforcement in the 1980s, and has gained widespread use. However the first appearance of what would now be termed designer drugs occurred well before this, in the 1920s.
Methamphetamine	Methamphetamine, methylamphetamine, N-methylamphetamine, desoxyephedrine, and colloquially as "meth" or "crystal meth", is a psychostimulant of the phenethylamine and amphetamine class of drugs. It increases alertness, concentration, energy, and in high doses, can induce euphoria, enhance self-esteem, and increase libido. Methamphetamine has high potential for abuse and addiction by activating the psychological reward system via triggering a cascading release of dopamine, norepinephrine and serotonin in the brain.
Narcolepsy	Narcolepsy is a chronic sleep disorder, or dyssomnia, characterized by excessive daytime sleepiness (EDS) in which a person experiences extreme fatigue and possibly falls asleep at inappropriate times, such as while at work or at school. Narcoleptics usually experience disturbed nocturnal sleep and an abnormal daytime sleep pattern, which is often confused with insomnia. When a narcoleptic falls asleep they generally experience the REM stage of sleep within 10 minutes; whereas most people do not experience REM sleep until after 90 minutes.

Chapter 1. PSYCHOACTIVE DRUGS: HISTORY & CLASSIFICATION

Psychiatric medication	A psychiatric medication is a licensed psychoactive drug taken to exert an effect on the mental state and used to treat mental disorders. Usually prescribed in psychiatric settings, these medications are typically made of synthetic chemical compounds, although some are naturally occurring, or at least naturally derived. Administration Prescription psychiatric medications, like all prescription medications, require a prescription from a physician, such as a psychiatrist, or a psychiatric nurse practitioner, PMHNP, before they can be obtained.
Psychopharmacology	Psychopharmacology is the study of drug-induced changes in mood, sensation, thinking, and behavior. The field of psychopharmacology studies a wide range of substances with various types of psychoactive properties. The professional and commercial fields of pharmacology and psychopharmacology do not mainly focus on psychedelic or recreational drugs, as the majority of studies are conducted for the development, study, and use of drugs for the modification of behavior and the alleviation of symptoms, particularly in the treatment of mental disorders (psychiatric medication).
Antipsychotic	An antipsychotic is a tranquilizing psychiatric medication primarily used to manage psychosis (including delusions or hallucinations, as well as disordered thought), particularly in schizophrenia and bipolar disorder. A first generation of antipsychotics, known as typical antipsychotics, was discovered in the 1950s. Most of the drugs in the second generation, known as atypical antipsychotics, have been developed more recently, although the first atypical antipsychotic, clozapine, was discovered in the 1950s and introduced clinically in the 1970s.
Chloral hydrate	Chloral hydrate is a sedative and hypnotic drug as well as a chemical reagent and precursor. The name chloral hydrate indicates that it is formed from chloral (trichloroacetaldehyde) by the addition of one molecule of water. Its chemical formula is $C_2H_3Cl_3O_2$.

Chapter 1. PSYCHOACTIVE DRUGS: HISTORY & CLASSIFICATION

Meprobamate	Meprobamate is a carbamate derivative which is used as an anxiolytic drug. It was the best-selling minor tranquilizer for a time, but has largely been replaced by the benzodiazepines. History Meprobamate was first synthesized by Bernard John Ludwig, PhD, and Frank Milan Berger, MD, at Carter Products in May 1950. Wallace Laboratories, a subsidiary of Carter Products, bought the license and named it Miltown after the borough of Milltown in New Jersey.
Serotonin	Serotonin is a monoamine neurotransmitter. Biochemically derived from tryptophan, serotonin is primarily found in the gastrointestinal (GI) tract, platelets, and in the central nervous system (CNS) of animals including humans. It is a well-known contributor to feelings of well-being; therefore it is also known as a "happiness hormone" despite not being a hormone.
Salvia divinorum	Salvia divinorum is a psychoactive plant which can induce dissociative effects and is a potent producer of "visions" and other hallucinatory experiences. Its native habitat is within cloud forest in the isolated Sierra Mazateca of Oaxaca, Mexico, growing in shady and moist locations. The plant grows to over a meter high, has hollow square stems, large leaves, and occasional white flowers with violet calyx.
Endorphin	Endorphins ("endogenous morphine") are endogenous opioid peptides that function as neurotransmitters. They are produced by the pituitary gland and the hypothalamus in vertebrates during exercise, excitement, pain, consumption of spicy food, love and orgasm, and they resemble the opiates in their abilities to produce analgesia and a feeling of well-being. The term "endorphin" implies a pharmacological activity (analogous to the activity of the corticosteroid category of biochemicals) as opposed to a specific chemical formulation.
Cathinone	Cathinone is chemically similar to ephedrine, cathine and other amphetamines. Cathinone induces the release of dopamine from striatal preparations that are prelabelled either with dopamine or its precursors. It is probably the main contributor to the stimulant effect of Catha edulis.

Chapter 1. PSYCHOACTIVE DRUGS: HISTORY & CLASSIFICATION

Codeine	Codeine (a natural isomer of methylated morphine, the other being the semi-synthetic 6-methylmorphine) is an opiate used for its analgesic, antitussive, and antidiarrheal properties. Codeine is the second-most predominant alkaloid in opium, at up to 3 percent; it is much more prevalent in the Iranian poppy (Papaver bractreatum), and codeine is extracted from this species in some places although the below-mentioned morphine methylation process is still much more common. It is considered the prototype of the weak to midrange opioids.
Oxycodone	Oxycodone is an opioid analgesic medication synthesized from opium-derived thebaine. It was developed in 1916 in Germany, as one of several new semi-synthetic opioids in an attempt to improve on the existing opioids: morphine, diacetylmorphine (heroin), and codeine. Oxycodone oral medications are generally prescribed for the relief of moderate to severe pain. Low dosages have also been prescribed for temporary relief of diarrhea. Currently it is formulated as single ingredient products or compounded products. Some common examples of compounding are oxycodone with acetaminophen/paracetamol or NSAIDs such as ibuprofen. The formulations are available as generics but are also made under various brand names.
Dopamine	Dopamine is a catecholamine neurotransmitter present in a wide variety of animals, including both vertebrates and invertebrates. In the brain, this substituted phenethylamine functions as a neurotransmitter, activating the five known types of dopamine receptors--D_1, D_2, D_3, D_4, and D_5--and their variants. Dopamine is produced in several areas of the brain, including the substantia nigra and the ventral tegmental area.
DEPRESSANT	Depressants are psychoactive drugs that temporarily reduce the function or activity of a specific part of the body or brain. Examples of these kinds of effects may include anxiolysis, sedation, and hypotension. Due to their effects typically having a "down" quality to them, depressants are also occasionally referred to as "downers".
Brainstem	In vertebrate anatomy the brainstem is the posterior part of the brain, adjoining and structurally continuous with the spinal cord. The brain stem provides the main motor and sensory innervation to the face and neck via the cranial nerves. Though small, this is an extremely important part of the brain as the nerve connections of the motor and sensory systems from the main part of the brain to the rest of the body pass through the brain stem.

Chapter 2. HEREDITY, ENVIRONMENT & PSYCHOACTIVE DRUGS

Narcotic	The term narcotic originally referred medically to any psychoactive compound with sleep-inducing properties. In the United States of America it has since become associated with opioids, commonly morphine and heroin. The term is, today, imprecisely defined and typically has negative connotations.
Neurotransmitter	Neurotransmitters are endogenous chemicals which transmit signals from a neuron to a target cell across a synapse. Neurotransmitters are packaged into synaptic vesicles clustered beneath the membrane on the presynaptic side of a synapse, and are released into the synaptic cleft, where they bind to receptors in the membrane on the postsynaptic side of the synapse. Release of neurotransmitters usually follows arrival of an action potential at the synapse, but may also follow graded electrical potentials.
MDMA	MDMA - colloquially known as ecstasy, often abbreviated "E" or "X" - is an entactogenic drug of the phenethylamine and amphetamine class of drugs. MDMA can induce euphoria, a sense of intimacy with others, and diminished anxiety and depression. Many, particularly in the fields of psychology and cognitive therapy, have suggested MDMA might have therapeutic benefits and facilitate therapy sessions in certain individuals, a practice which it had formally been used for in the past.
Morpheus	Morpheus in Greek mythology is the god of dreams, leader of the Oneiroi. Morpheus has the ability to take any human form and appear in dreams. His true semblance is that of a winged daemon, imagery shared with many of his siblings.
Opium	Opium is the dried latex obtained from the opium poppy (Papaver somniferum). Opium contains up to 12% morphine, an alkaloid, which is frequently processed chemically to produce heroin for the illegal drug trade. The latex also includes codeine and non-narcotic alkaloids such as papaverine, thebaine and noscapine.
Alcohol	In chemistry, an alcohol is any organic compound in which a hydroxyl functional group (-OH) is bound to a carbon atom, usually connected to other carbon or hydrogen atoms. An important class are the simple acyclic alcohols, the general formula for which is $C_nH_{2n+1}OH$. Of those, ethanol (C_2H_5OH) is the type of alcohol found in alcoholic beverages, and in common speech the word alcohol refers specifically to ethanol.

Chapter 2. HEREDITY, ENVIRONMENT & PSYCHOACTIVE DRUGS

Morphine	Supplementary data for morphine. Structure and properties
Naltrexone	Naltrexone is an opioid receptor antagonist used primarily in the management of alcohol dependence and opioid dependence. It is marketed in generic form as its hydrochloride salt, naltrexone hydrochloride, and marketed under the trade names Revia and Depade. In some countries including the United States, a once-monthly extended-release injectable formulation is marketed under the trade name Vivitrol. Also in the US, Methylnaltrexone Bromide, a closely related drug, is marketed as Relistor, for the treatment of opioid induced constipation.
Opioid	An opioid is a chemical that works by binding to opioid receptors, which are found principally in the central and peripheral nervous system and the gastrointestinal tract. The receptors in these organ systems mediate both the beneficial effects and the side effects of opioids. Opioids are among the world's oldest known drugs; the use of the opium poppy for its therapeutic benefits predates recorded history.
Oxycodone	Oxycodone is an opioid analgesic medication synthesized from opium-derived thebaine. It was developed in 1916 in Germany, as one of several new semi-synthetic opioids in an attempt to improve on the existing opioids: morphine, diacetylmorphine (heroin), and codeine. Oxycodone oral medications are generally prescribed for the relief of moderate to severe pain. Low dosages have also been prescribed for temporary relief of diarrhea. Currently it is formulated as single ingredient products or compounded products. Some common examples of compounding are oxycodone with acetaminophen/paracetamol or NSAIDs such as ibuprofen. The formulations are available as generics but are also made under various brand names.
Tranquilizer	A tranquilizer, is a drug that induces tranquillity in an individual.

Chapter 2. HEREDITY, ENVIRONMENT & PSYCHOACTIVE DRUGS

The term "tranquilizer" is imprecise, and is usually qualified, or replaced with more precise terms:

- minor tranquilizer usually refers to anxiolytic or antianxiety agent

- major tranquilizer usually refers to antipsychotics

Antimanic agents can also be considered tranquilizing agents.

In music

- "Tranquilizer" is a song written by Tom Stephan ' Neil Tennant, from album Superchumbo "WowieZowie" (2005).

- Tranquilizer by Fat Jon The Ample Soul Physician, from album Repaint Tomorow

.

Cocaine

Cocaine benzoylmethylecgonine (INN) is a crystalline tropane alkaloid that is obtained from the leaves of the coca plant. The name comes from "coca" in addition to the alkaloid suffix -ine, forming cocaine. It is a stimulant of the central nervous system, an appetite suppressant, and a topical anesthetic. Specifically, it is a serotonin-norepinephrine-dopamine reuptake inhibitor, which mediates functionality of these neurotransmitters as an exogenous catecholamine transporter ligand. Because of the way it affects the mesolimbic reward pathway, cocaine is addictive.

Serotonin

Serotonin is a monoamine neurotransmitter. Biochemically derived from tryptophan, serotonin is primarily found in the gastrointestinal (GI) tract, platelets, and in the central nervous system (CNS) of animals including humans. It is a well-known contributor to feelings of well-being; therefore it is also known as a "happiness hormone" despite not being a hormone.

Cannabis

Cannabis is a genus of flowering plants that includes three putative species, Cannabis sativa, Cannabis indica, and Cannabis ruderalis. These three taxa are indigenous to Central Asia, and South Asia. Cannabis has long been used for fibre (hemp), for seed and seed oils, for medicinal purposes, and as a recreational drug.

Ketamine

Ketamine is a drug used in human and veterinary medicine. Its hydrochloride salt is sold as Ketanest, Ketaset, and Ketalar. Pharmacologically, ketamine is classified as an NMDA receptor antagonist.

Chapter 2. HEREDITY, ENVIRONMENT & PSYCHOACTIVE DRUGS

Fluoxetine	Fluoxetine is an antidepressant of the selective serotonin reuptake inhibitor (SSRI) class. It is manufactured and marketed by Eli Lilly and Company. In combination with olanzapine it is known as symbyax. Fluoxetine is approved for the treatment of major depression (including pediatric depression), obsessive-compulsive disorder (in both adult and pediatric populations), bulimia nervosa, panic disorder and premenstrual dysphoric disorder.
Salvia divinorum	Salvia divinorum is a psychoactive plant which can induce dissociative effects and is a potent producer of "visions" and other hallucinatory experiences. Its native habitat is within cloud forest in the isolated Sierra Mazateca of Oaxaca, Mexico, growing in shady and moist locations. The plant grows to over a meter high, has hollow square stems, large leaves, and occasional white flowers with violet calyx.
Brainstem	In vertebrate anatomy the brainstem is the posterior part of the brain, adjoining and structurally continuous with the spinal cord. The brain stem provides the main motor and sensory innervation to the face and neck via the cranial nerves. Though small, this is an extremely important part of the brain as the nerve connections of the motor and sensory systems from the main part of the brain to the rest of the body pass through the brain stem.
Substance abuse	Substance abuse refers to a maladaptive pattern of use of a substance that is not considered dependent. The term "drug abuse" does not exclude dependency, but is otherwise used in a similar manner in nonmedical contexts. The terms have a huge range of definitions related to taking a psychoactive drug or performance enhancing drug for a non-therapeutic or non-medical effect.
Endorphin	Endorphins ("endogenous morphine") are endogenous opioid peptides that function as neurotransmitters. They are produced by the pituitary gland and the hypothalamus in vertebrates during exercise, excitement, pain, consumption of spicy food, love and orgasm, and they resemble the opiates in their abilities to produce analgesia and a feeling of well-being. The term "endorphin" implies a pharmacological activity (analogous to the activity of the corticosteroid category of biochemicals) as opposed to a specific chemical formulation.
Hypothalamus	The Hypothalamus is a portion of the brain that contains a number of small nuclei with a variety of functions. One of the most important functions of the hypothalamus is to link the nervous system to the endocrine system via the pituitary gland (hypophysis).

	The hypothalamus is located below the thalamus, just above the brain stem.
Sympathetic nervous system	The (ortho-) sympathetic nervous system is one of the three parts of the autonomic nervous system, along with the enteric and parasympathetic systems. Its general action is to mobilize the body's resources under stress; to induce the fight-or-flight response. It is, however, constantly active at a basal level in order to maintain homeostasis.
Depression	Depression, one of the most commonly diagnosed psychiatric disorders, is being diagnosed in increasing numbers in various segments of the population worldwide. Depression in the United States alone affects 17.6 million Americans each year or 1 in 6 people. Depressed patients are at increased risk of type 2 diabetes, cardiovascular disease and suicide. Within the next twenty years depression is expected to become the second leading cause of disability worldwide and the leading cause in high-income nations, including the United States. In approximately 75% of completed suicides the individuals had seen a physician within the prior year before their death, 45%-66% within the prior month. Approximately 33% - 41% of those who completed suicide had contact with mental health services in the prior year, 20% within the prior month.
Limbic system	The limbic system is a set of brain structures including the hippocampus, amygdala, anterior thalamic nuclei, septum, limbic cortex and fornix, which seemingly support a variety of functions including emotion, behavior, long term memory, and olfaction. The term "limbic" comes from the Latin limbus, for "border" or "edge". Some scientists have suggested that the concept of the limbic system should be abandoned as obsolete, as it is grounded more in transient tradition than in facts.
Amygdala	The amygdalae are almond-shaped groups of nuclei located deep within the medial temporal lobes of the brain in complex vertebrates, including humans. Shown in research to perform a primary role in the processing and memory of emotional reactions, the amygdalae are considered part of the limbic system.
Dopamine	Dopamine is a catecholamine neurotransmitter present in a wide variety of animals, including both vertebrates and invertebrates. In the brain, this substituted phenethylamine functions as a neurotransmitter, activating the five known types of dopamine receptors--D_1, D_2, D_3, D_4, and D_5--and their variants. Dopamine is produced in several areas of the brain, including the substantia nigra and the ventral tegmental area.

Chapter 2. HEREDITY, ENVIRONMENT & PSYCHOACTIVE DRUGS

Dopaminergic	Dopaminergic means related to the neurotransmitter dopamine. For example, certain proteins such as the dopamine transporter (DAT), vesicular monoamine transporter 2 ($VMAT_2$), and dopamine receptors can be classified as dopaminergic, and neurons which synthesize or contain dopamine and synapses with dopamine receptors in them may also be labeled as dopaminergic. Enzymes which regulate the biosynthesis or metabolism of dopamine such as aromatic L-amino acid decarboxylase (AAAD) or DOPA decarboxylase (DDC), monoamine oxidase (MAO), and catechol O-methyl transferase (COMT) may be referred to as dopaminergic as well.
Nucleus accumbens	The nucleus accumbens also known as the accumbens nucleus or as the nucleus accumbens septi, is a collection of neurons within the striatum. It is thought to play an important role in reward, pleasure, laughter, addiction, aggression, fear, and the placebo effect. Each half of the brain has one nucleus accumbens.
Acetylcholine	The chemical compound acetylcholine is a neurotransmitter in both the peripheral nervous system (PNS) and central nervous system (CNS) in many organisms including humans. Acetylcholine is one of many neurotransmitters in the autonomic nervous system (ANS) and the only neurotransmitter used in the motor division of the somatic nervous system. (Sensory neurons use glutamate and various peptides at their synapses). Acetylcholine is also the principal neurotransmitter in all autonomic ganglia.
Norepinephrine	Norepinephrine is a catecholamine with multiple roles including as a hormone and a neurotransmitter. As a stress hormone, norepinephrine affects parts of the brain, such as the amygdala, where attention and responses are controlled. Along with epinephrine, norepinephrine also underlies the fight-or-flight response, directly increasing heart rate, triggering the release of glucose from energy stores, and increasing blood flow to skeletal muscle. It increases the brain's oxygen supply. Norepinephrine can also suppress neuroinflammation when released diffusely in the brain from the locus ceruleus.
Epinephrine	Epinephrine is a hormone and a neurotransmitter. It increases heart rate, constricts blood vessels, dilates air passages and participates in the fight-or-flight response of the sympathetic nervous system. Chemically, epinephrine is a catecholamine, a monoamine produced only by the adrenal glands from the amino acids phenylalanine and tyrosine.

Chapter 2. HEREDITY, ENVIRONMENT & PSYCHOACTIVE DRUGS

Hallucination	A hallucination, in the broadest sense of the word, is a perception in the absence of a stimulus. In a stricter sense, hallucinations are defined as perceptions in a conscious and awake state in the absence of external stimuli which have qualities of real perception, in that they are vivid, substantial, and located in external objective space. The latter definition distinguishes hallucinations from the related phenomena of dreaming, which does not involve wakefulness; illusion, which involves distorted or misinterpreted real perception; imagery, which does not mimic real perception and is under voluntary control; and pseudohallucination, which does not mimic real perception, but is not under voluntary control.
Stimulant	Stimulants are psychoactive drugs which induce temporary improvements in either mental or physical function or both. Examples of these kinds of effects may include enhanced alertness, wakefulness, and locomotion, among others. Due to their effects typically having an "up" quality to them, stimulants are also occasionally referred to as "uppers".
Methamphetamine	Methamphetamine, methylamphetamine, N-methylamphetamine, desoxyephedrine, and colloquially as "meth" or "crystal meth", is a psychostimulant of the phenethylamine and amphetamine class of drugs. It increases alertness, concentration, energy, and in high doses, can induce euphoria, enhance self-esteem, and increase libido. Methamphetamine has high potential for abuse and addiction by activating the psychological reward system via triggering a cascading release of dopamine, norepinephrine and serotonin in the brain.
Catecholamine	Catecholamines are "fight-or-flight" hormones released by the adrenal glands in response to stress. They are part of the sympathetic nervous system. They are called catecholamines because they contain a catechol or 3,4-dihydroxylphenyl group.
Hormone	A hormone is a chemical released by a cell or a gland in one part of the body that sends out messages that affect cells in other parts of the organism. Only a small amount of hormone is required to alter cell metabolism. In essence, it is a chemical messenger that transports a signal from one cell to another. All multicellular organisms produce hormones; plant hormones are also called phytohormones. Hormones in animals are often transported in the blood. Cells respond to a hormone when they express a specific receptor for that hormone. The hormone binds to the receptor protein, resulting in the activation of a signal transduction mechanism that ultimately leads to cell type-specific responses.
Opioid peptide	Opioid peptides are short sequences of amino acids that bind to opioid receptors in the brain; opiates and opioids mimic the effect of these peptides. Opioid peptides may be produced by the body itself, for example endorphins. The effects of these peptides vary, but they all resemble opiates.

Chapter 2. HEREDITY, ENVIRONMENT & PSYCHOACTIVE DRUGS

Psychoactive drug	A psychoactive drug, psychopharmaceutical, or psychotropic is a chemical substance that crosses the blood-brain barrier and acts primarily upon the central nervous system where it affects brain function, resulting in changes in perception, mood, consciousness, cognition, and behavior. These substances may be used recreationally, to purposefully alter one's consciousness, as entheogens, for ritual, spiritual, and/or shamanic purposes, as a tool for studying or augmenting the mind, or therapeutically as medication. Because psychoactive substances bring about subjective changes in consciousness and mood that the user may find pleasant (e.g. euphoria) or advantageous (e.g. increased alertness), many psychoactive substances are abused, that is, used excessively, despite the health risks or negative consequences.
Ibogaine	Ibogaine is a naturally occurring psychoactive substance found in a number of plants, principally in a member of the Apocynaceae family known as iboga (Tabernanthe iboga). A hallucinogen, the substance is banned in some countries; in other countries it is being used to treat addiction to opiates, methamphetamine and other drugs. Derivatives of ibogaine that lack the substance's hallucinogen properties are under development.
Kava	Kava is a crop of the western Pacific. The roots of the plant are used to produce a drink with mild sedative properties. Kava is consumed throughout the Pacific Ocean cultures of Polynesia (including Hawaii), Vanuatu, Melanesia and some parts of Micronesia. Kava is sedating and is primarily consumed to relax without disrupting mental clarity. Its active ingredients are called kavalactones.
Khat	Khat is a flowering plant native to tropical East Africa and the Arabian Peninsula. Khat contains the alkaloid called cathinone, an amphetamine-like stimulant which is said to cause excitement, loss of appetite, and euphoria. In 1980, the World Health Organization classified khat as a drug of abuse that can produce mild to moderate psychological dependence (less than tobacco or alcohol). The plant has been targeted by anti-drug organizations like the DEA. It is a controlled or illegal substance in many countries, but is legal for sale and production in many others.

Chapter 2. HEREDITY, ENVIRONMENT & PSYCHOACTIVE DRUGS

BARBITURATE	Barbiturates are drugs that act as central nervous system depressants, and, by virtue of this, they produce a wide spectrum of effects, from mild sedation to total anesthesia. They are also effective as anxiolytics, as hypnotics, and as anticonvulsants. They have addiction potential, both physical and psychological. Barbiturates have now largely been replaced by benzodiazepines in routine medical practice - for example, in the treatment of anxiety and insomnia - mainly because benzodiazepines are significantly less dangerous in overdose. However, barbiturates are still used in general anesthesia, as well as for epilepsy. Barbiturates are derivatives of barbituric acid.
Codeine	Codeine (a natural isomer of methylated morphine, the other being the semi-synthetic 6-methylmorphine) is an opiate used for its analgesic, antitussive, and antidiarrheal properties. Codeine is the second-most predominant alkaloid in opium, at up to 3 percent; it is much more prevalent in the Iranian poppy (Papaver bractreatum), and codeine is extracted from this species in some places although the below-mentioned morphine methylation process is still much more common. It is considered the prototype of the weak to midrange opioids.
Clonidine	Clonidine is a medication used to treat several medical conditions. It is a direct-acting α_2 adrenergic agonist and an imidazoline. It has been prescribed historically as an antihypertensive drug. It has found new uses, including treatment of some types of neuropathic pain, opioid detoxification, sleep hyperhidrosis, anaesthetic use, and off-label, to counter the side effects of stimulant medications such as methylphenidate or amphetamine. It is becoming a more accepted treatment for insomnia, as well as for relief of menopausal symptoms.
Psychiatric medication	A psychiatric medication is a licensed psychoactive drug taken to exert an effect on the mental state and used to treat mental disorders. Usually prescribed in psychiatric settings, these medications are typically made of synthetic chemical compounds, although some are naturally occurring, or at least naturally derived. Administration Prescription psychiatric medications, like all prescription medications, require a prescription from a physician, such as a psychiatrist, or a psychiatric nurse practitioner, PMHNP, before they can be obtained.

Chapter 2. HEREDITY, ENVIRONMENT & PSYCHOACTIVE DRUGS

Psychopharmacology	Psychopharmacology is the study of drug-induced changes in mood, sensation, thinking, and behavior.
	The field of psychopharmacology studies a wide range of substances with various types of psychoactive properties. The professional and commercial fields of pharmacology and psychopharmacology do not mainly focus on psychedelic or recreational drugs, as the majority of studies are conducted for the development, study, and use of drugs for the modification of behavior and the alleviation of symptoms, particularly in the treatment of mental disorders (psychiatric medication).
Desipramine	Desipramine is a tricyclic antidepressant (TCA). It inhibits the reuptake of norepinephrine and to a lesser extent serotonin. It is used to treat depression, but not considered a first line treatment since the introduction of SSRI antidepressants. Desipramine is an active metabolite of imipramine.
Speedball	Speedball is a term commonly referring to the hazardous intravenous use of heroin and cocaine together in the same syringe.
	Cocaine acts as a stimulant, whereas heroin acts as a depressant. Coadministration provides an intense rush of euphoria with a high that combines both effects of the drugs, while excluding the negative effects, such as anxiety and sedation.
Posttraumatic stress disorder	Posttraumatic stress disorder is a severe anxiety disorder that can develop after exposure to any event that results in psychological trauma. This event may involve the threat of death to oneself or to someone else, or to one's own or someone else's physical, sexual, or psychological integrity, overwhelming the individual's ability to cope. As an effect of psychological trauma, Posttraumatic stress disorder is less frequent and more enduring than the more commonly seen acute stress response.

Chapter 2. HEREDITY, ENVIRONMENT & PSYCHOACTIVE DRUGS

Antipsychotic	An antipsychotic is a tranquilizing psychiatric medication primarily used to manage psychosis (including delusions or hallucinations, as well as disordered thought), particularly in schizophrenia and bipolar disorder. A first generation of antipsychotics, known as typical antipsychotics, was discovered in the 1950s. Most of the drugs in the second generation, known as atypical antipsychotics, have been developed more recently, although the first atypical antipsychotic, clozapine, was discovered in the 1950s and introduced clinically in the 1970s.
Long-term potentiation	In neuroscience, long-term potentiation is a long-lasting enhancement in signal transmission between two neurons that results from stimulating them synchronously. It is one of several phenomena underlying synaptic plasticity, the ability of chemical synapses to change their strength. As memories are thought to be encoded by modification of synaptic strength, Long term potentiation is widely considered one of the major cellular mechanisms that underlies learning and memory.

41

Chapter 3. UPPERS

STIMULANT	Stimulants are psychoactive drugs which induce temporary improvements in either mental or physical function or both. Examples of these kinds of effects may include enhanced alertness, wakefulness, and locomotion, among others. Due to their effects typically having an "up" quality to them, stimulants are also occasionally referred to as "uppers".
COCAINE	Cocaine benzoylmethylecgonine (INN) is a crystalline tropane alkaloid that is obtained from the leaves of the coca plant. The name comes from "coca" in addition to the alkaloid suffix -ine, forming cocaine. It is a stimulant of the central nervous system, an appetite suppressant, and a topical anesthetic. Specifically, it is a serotonin-norepinephrine-dopamine reuptake inhibitor, which mediates functionality of these neurotransmitters as an exogenous catecholamine transporter ligand. Because of the way it affects the mesolimbic reward pathway, cocaine is addictive.
Khat	Khat is a flowering plant native to tropical East Africa and the Arabian Peninsula. Khat contains the alkaloid called cathinone, an amphetamine-like stimulant which is said to cause excitement, loss of appetite, and euphoria. In 1980, the World Health Organization classified khat as a drug of abuse that can produce mild to moderate psychological dependence (less than tobacco or alcohol). The plant has been targeted by anti-drug organizations like the DEA. It is a controlled or illegal substance in many countries, but is legal for sale and production in many others.
MDMA	MDMA - colloquially known as ecstasy, often abbreviated "E" or "X" - is an entactogenic drug of the phenethylamine and amphetamine class of drugs. MDMA can induce euphoria, a sense of intimacy with others, and diminished anxiety and depression. Many, particularly in the fields of psychology and cognitive therapy, have suggested MDMA might have therapeutic benefits and facilitate therapy sessions in certain individuals, a practice which it had formally been used for in the past.

Chapter 3. UPPERS

Designer drug	Designer drug is a term used to describe drugs which are created (or marketed, if they had already existed) to get around existing drug laws, usually by modifying the molecular structures of existing drugs to varying degrees, or less commonly by finding drugs with entirely different chemical structures that produce similar subjective effects to illegal recreational drugs. History United States 1920s-1930s The term "designer drug" was first coined by law enforcement in the 1980s, and has gained widespread use. However the first appearance of what would now be termed designer drugs occurred well before this, in the 1920s.
Methamphetamine	Methamphetamine, methylamphetamine, N-methylamphetamine, desoxyephedrine, and colloquially as "meth" or "crystal meth", is a psychostimulant of the phenethylamine and amphetamine class of drugs. It increases alertness, concentration, energy, and in high doses, can induce euphoria, enhance self-esteem, and increase libido. Methamphetamine has high potential for abuse and addiction by activating the psychological reward system via triggering a cascading release of dopamine, norepinephrine and serotonin in the brain.
Methylphenidate	Methylphenidate is a psychostimulant drug approved for treatment of attention-deficit hyperactivity disorder, postural orthostatic tachycardia syndrome, and narcolepsy. It may also be prescribed for off-label use in treatment-resistant cases of lethargy, depression, neural insult, obesity, and rarely other psychiatric disorders such as obsessive-compulsive disorder. Methylphenidate belongs to the piperidine class of compounds and increases the levels of dopamine and norepinephrine in the brain through reuptake inhibition of the monoamine transporters. It also increases the release of dopamine and norepinephrine. MPH possesses structural similarities to amphetamine, and, though it is less potent, its pharmacological effects are even more closely related to those of cocaine.

Chapter 3. UPPERS

Modafinil	Modafinil is an analeptic drug manufactured by Cephalon, and is approved by the U.S. Food and Drug Administration (FDA) for the treatment of narcolepsy, shift work sleep disorder, and excessive daytime sleepiness associated with obstructive sleep apnea. The European Medicines Agency has recommended that in Europe it be prescribed only for narcolepsy.
Phenylephrine	Phenylephrine is a selective α1-adrenergic receptor agonist used primarily as a decongestant, as an agent to dilate the pupil, and to increase blood pressure. Phenylephrine has recently been marketed as a substitute for pseudoephedrine (e.g.,Sudafed (Original Formulation)), but there are recent claims that oral phenylephrine may be no more effective as a decongestant than a placebo .
	Uses
	Decongestant
	Phenylephrine is used as a decongestant sold as an oral medicine, as a nasal spray, or as eye drops.
Phenylpropanolamine	Phenylpropanolamine is a psychoactive drug of the phenethylamine and amphetamine chemical classes which is used as a stimulant, decongestant, and anorectic agent. It is commonly used in prescription and over-the-counter cough and cold preparations. In veterinary medicine, it is used to control urinary incontinence in dogs under trade names Propalin and Proin.
Sibutramine	Sibutramine is an oral anorexiant. Until recently it was marketed and prescribed as an adjunct in the treatment of exogenous obesity along with diet and exercise. It has been associated with increased cardiovascular events and strokes and has been withdrawn from the market in the United States, the UK, the EU, Australia, Canada, Hong Kong, Thailand and Mexico and recently in India following the decision of an expert committee on its effects on CVS (SCOUT report).
NEUROTRANSMITTER	Neurotransmitters are endogenous chemicals which transmit signals from a neuron to a target ce across a synapse. Neurotransmitters are packaged into synaptic vesicles clustered beneath the membrane on the presynaptic side of a synapse, and are released into the synaptic cleft, where they bind to receptors in the membrane on the postsynaptic side of the synapse. Release of neurotransmitters usually follows arrival of an action potential at the synapse, but may also follov graded electrical potentials.

Chapter 3. UPPERS

Alcohol	In chemistry, an alcohol is any organic compound in which a hydroxyl functional group (-OH) is bound to a carbon atom, usually connected to other carbon or hydrogen atoms. An important class are the simple acyclic alcohols, the general formula for which is $C_nH_{2n+1}OH$. Of those, ethanol (C_2H_5OH) is the type of alcohol found in alcoholic beverages, and in common speech the word alcohol refers specifically to ethanol.
Brainstem	In vertebrate anatomy the brainstem is the posterior part of the brain, adjoining and structurally continuous with the spinal cord. The brain stem provides the main motor and sensory innervation to the face and neck via the cranial nerves. Though small, this is an extremely important part of the brain as the nerve connections of the motor and sensory systems from the main part of the brain to the rest of the body pass through the brain stem.
Cathinone	Cathinone is chemically similar to ephedrine, cathine and other amphetamines. Cathinone induces the release of dopamine from striatal preparations that are prelabelled either with dopamine or its precursors. It is probably the main contributor to the stimulant effect of Catha edulis.
Dopamine	Dopamine is a catecholamine neurotransmitter present in a wide variety of animals, including both vertebrates and invertebrates. In the brain, this substituted phenethylamine functions as a neurotransmitter, activating the five known types of dopamine receptors--D_1, D_2, D_3, D_4, and D_5-- and their variants. Dopamine is produced in several areas of the brain, including the substantia nigra and the ventral tegmental area.
Epinephrine	Epinephrine is a hormone and a neurotransmitter. It increases heart rate, constricts blood vessels, dilates air passages and participates in the fight-or-flight response of the sympathetic nervous system. Chemically, epinephrine is a catecholamine, a monoamine produced only by the adrenal glands from the amino acids phenylalanine and tyrosine.
Hormone	A hormone is a chemical released by a cell or a gland in one part of the body that sends out messages that affect cells in other parts of the organism. Only a small amount of hormone is required to alter cell metabolism. In essence, it is a chemical messenger that transports a signal from one cell to another. All multicellular organisms produce hormones; plant hormones are also called phytohormones. Hormones in animals are often transported in the blood. Cells respond to a hormone when they express a specific receptor for that hormone. The hormone binds to the receptor protein, resulting in the activation of a signal transduction mechanism that ultimately leads to cell type-specific responses.

Chapter 3. UPPERS

Ketamine	Ketamine is a drug used in human and veterinary medicine. Its hydrochloride salt is sold as Ketanest, Ketaset, and Ketalar. Pharmacologically, ketamine is classified as an NMDA receptor antagonist.
Narcolepsy	Narcolepsy is a chronic sleep disorder, or dyssomnia, characterized by excessive daytime sleepiness (EDS) in which a person experiences extreme fatigue and possibly falls asleep at inappropriate times, such as while at work or at school. Narcoleptics usually experience disturbed nocturnal sleep and an abnormal daytime sleep pattern, which is often confused with insomnia. When a narcoleptic falls asleep they generally experience the REM stage of sleep within 10 minutes; whereas most people do not experience REM sleep until after 90 minutes.
Norepinephrine	Norepinephrine is a catecholamine with multiple roles including as a hormone and a neurotransmitter. As a stress hormone, norepinephrine affects parts of the brain, such as the amygdala, where attention and responses are controlled. Along with epinephrine, norepinephrine also underlies the fight-or-flight response, directly increasing heart rate, triggering the release of glucose from energy stores, and increasing blood flow to skeletal muscle. It increases the brain's oxygen supply. Norepinephrine can also suppress neuroinflammation when released diffusely in the brain from the locus ceruleus.
Serotonin	Serotonin is a monoamine neurotransmitter. Biochemically derived from tryptophan, serotonin is primarily found in the gastrointestinal (GI) tract, platelets, and in the central nervous system (CNS) of animals including humans. It is a well-known contributor to feelings of well-being; therefore it is also known as a "happiness hormone" despite not being a hormone.
Psychoactive drug	A psychoactive drug, psychopharmaceutical, or psychotropic is a chemical substance that crosses the blood-brain barrier and acts primarily upon the central nervous system where it affects brain function, resulting in changes in perception, mood, consciousness, cognition, and behavior. These substances may be used recreationally, to purposefully alter one's consciousness, as entheogens, for ritual, spiritual, and/or shamanic purposes, as a tool for studying or augmenting the mind, or therapeutically as medication.

Chapter 3. UPPERS

	Because psychoactive substances bring about subjective changes in consciousness and mood that the user may find pleasant (e.g. euphoria) or advantageous (e.g. increased alertness), many psychoactive substances are abused, that is, used excessively, despite the health risks or negative consequences.
Substance abuse	Substance abuse refers to a maladaptive pattern of use of a substance that is not considered dependent. The term "drug abuse" does not exclude dependency, but is otherwise used in a similar manner in nonmedical contexts. The terms have a huge range of definitions related to taking a psychoactive drug or performance enhancing drug for a non-therapeutic or non-medical effect.
Amygdala	The amygdalae are almond-shaped groups of nuclei located deep within the medial temporal lobes of the brain in complex vertebrates, including humans. Shown in research to perform a primary role in the processing and memory of emotional reactions, the amygdalae are considered part of the limbic system.
Hypothalamus	The Hypothalamus is a portion of the brain that contains a number of small nuclei with a variety of functions. One of the most important functions of the hypothalamus is to link the nervous system to the endocrine system via the pituitary gland (hypophysis). The hypothalamus is located below the thalamus, just above the brain stem.
Psychiatric medication	A psychiatric medication is a licensed psychoactive drug taken to exert an effect on the mental state and used to treat mental disorders. Usually prescribed in psychiatric settings, these medications are typically made of synthetic chemical compounds, although some are naturally occurring, or at least naturally derived. Administration Prescription psychiatric medications, like all prescription medications, require a prescription from a physician, such as a psychiatrist, or a psychiatric nurse practitioner, PMHNP, before they can be obtained.

Chapter 3. UPPERS

Psychopharmacology	Psychopharmacology is the study of drug-induced changes in mood, sensation, thinking, and behavior.
	The field of psychopharmacology studies a wide range of substances with various types of psychoactive properties. The professional and commercial fields of pharmacology and psychopharmacology do not mainly focus on psychedelic or recreational drugs, as the majority of studies are conducted for the development, study, and use of drugs for the modification of behavior and the alleviation of symptoms, particularly in the treatment of mental disorders (psychiatric medication).
Salvia divinorum	Salvia divinorum is a psychoactive plant which can induce dissociative effects and is a potent producer of "visions" and other hallucinatory experiences. Its native habitat is within cloud forest in the isolated Sierra Mazateca of Oaxaca, Mexico, growing in shady and moist locations. The plant grows to over a meter high, has hollow square stems, large leaves, and occasional white flowers with violet calyx.
Ibogaine	Ibogaine is a naturally occurring psychoactive substance found in a number of plants, principally in a member of the Apocynaceae family known as iboga (Tabernanthe iboga).
	A hallucinogen, the substance is banned in some countries; in other countries it is being used to treat addiction to opiates, methamphetamine and other drugs. Derivatives of ibogaine that lack the substance's hallucinogen properties are under development.
Kava	Kava is a crop of the western Pacific. The roots of the plant are used to produce a drink with mild sedative properties. Kava is consumed throughout the Pacific Ocean cultures of Polynesia (including Hawaii), Vanuatu, Melanesia and some parts of Micronesia. Kava is sedating and is primarily consumed to relax without disrupting mental clarity. Its active ingredients are called kavalactones.
Nucleus accumbens	The nucleus accumbens also known as the accumbens nucleus or as the nucleus accumbens septi, is a collection of neurons within the striatum. It is thought to play an important role in reward, pleasure, laughter, addiction, aggression, fear, and the placebo effect.

	Each half of the brain has one nucleus accumbens.
Opium	Opium is the dried latex obtained from the opium poppy (Papaver somniferum). Opium contains up to 12% morphine, an alkaloid, which is frequently processed chemically to produce heroin for the illegal drug trade. The latex also includes codeine and non-narcotic alkaloids such as papaverine, thebaine and noscapine.
Morpheus	Morpheus in Greek mythology is the god of dreams, leader of the Oneiroi. Morpheus has the ability to take any human form and appear in dreams. His true semblance is that of a winged daemon, imagery shared with many of his siblings.
Narcotic	The term narcotic originally referred medically to any psychoactive compound with sleep-inducing properties. In the United States of America it has since become associated with opioids, commonly morphine and heroin. The term is, today, imprecisely defined and typically has negative connotations.
Morphine	Supplementary data for morphine. Structure and properties
Acetylcholine	The chemical compound acetylcholine is a neurotransmitter in both the peripheral nervous system (PNS) and central nervous system (CNS) in many organisms including humans. Acetylcholine is one of many neurotransmitters in the autonomic nervous system (ANS) and the only neurotransmitter used in the motor division of the somatic nervous system. (Sensory neurons use glutamate and various peptides at their synapses). Acetylcholine is also the principal neurotransmitter in all autonomic ganglia.
Catecholamine	Catecholamines are "fight-or-flight" hormones released by the adrenal glands in response to stress. They are part of the sympathetic nervous system. They are called catecholamines because they contain a catechol or 3,4-dihydroxylphenyl group.

Chapter 3. UPPERS

Limbic system	The limbic system is a set of brain structures including the hippocampus, amygdala, anterior thalamic nuclei, septum, limbic cortex and fornix, which seemingly support a variety of functions including emotion, behavior, long term memory, and olfaction. The term "limbic" comes from the Latin limbus, for "border" or "edge". Some scientists have suggested that the concept of the limbic system should be abandoned as obsolete, as it is grounded more in transient tradition than in facts.
Sympathetic nervous system	The (ortho-) sympathetic nervous system is one of the three parts of the autonomic nervous system, along with the enteric and parasympathetic systems. Its general action is to mobilize the body's resources under stress; to induce the fight-or-flight response. It is, however, constantly active at a basal level in order to maintain homeostasis.
Cannabis	Cannabis is a genus of flowering plants that includes three putative species, Cannabis sativa, Cannabis indica, and Cannabis ruderalis. These three taxa are indigenous to Central Asia, and South Asia. Cannabis has long been used for fibre (hemp), for seed and seed oils, for medicinal purposes, and as a recreational drug.
Hallucination	A hallucination, in the broadest sense of the word, is a perception in the absence of a stimulus. In a stricter sense, hallucinations are defined as perceptions in a conscious and awake state in the absence of external stimuli which have qualities of real perception, in that they are vivid, substantial, and located in external objective space. The latter definition distinguishes hallucinations from the related phenomena of dreaming, which does not involve wakefulness; illusion, which involves distorted or misinterpreted real perception; imagery, which does not mimic real perception and is under voluntary control; and pseudohallucination, which does not mimic real perception, but is not under voluntary control.
Speedball	Speedball is a term commonly referring to the hazardous intravenous use of heroin and cocaine together in the same syringe. Cocaine acts as a stimulant, whereas heroin acts as a depressant. Coadministration provides an intense rush of euphoria with a high that combines both effects of the drugs, while excluding the negative effects, such as anxiety and sedation.

Chapter 3. UPPERS

Decongestant	A decongestant is a type of drug that is used to relieve nasal congestion. The vast majority of decongestants act via enhancing norepinephrine (noradrenaline) and epinephrine (adrenaline) or adrenergic activity by stimulating the α-adrenergic receptors. This induces vasoconstriction of the blood vessels in the nose, throat, and paranasal sinuses, which results in reduced inflammation (swelling) and mucus formation in these areas.
Depression	Depression, one of the most commonly diagnosed psychiatric disorders, is being diagnosed in increasing numbers in various segments of the population worldwide. Depression in the United States alone affects 17.6 million Americans each year or 1 in 6 people. Depressed patients are at increased risk of type 2 diabetes, cardiovascular disease and suicide. Within the next twenty years depression is expected to become the second leading cause of disability worldwide and the leading cause in high-income nations, including the United States. In approximately 75% of completed suicides the individuals had seen a physician within the prior year before their death, 45%-66% within the prior month. Approximately 33% - 41% of those who completed suicide had contact with mental health services in the prior year, 20% within the prior month.
Major depressive disorder	Major depressive disorder is a mental disorder characterized by an all-encompassing low mood accompanied by low self-esteem, and by loss of interest or pleasure in normally enjoyable activities. This cluster of symptoms (syndrome) was named, described and classified as one of the mood disorders in the 1980 edition of the American Psychiatric Association's diagnostic manual. The term "depression" is ambiguous. It is often used to denote this syndrome but may refer to any or all of the mood disorders. Major depressive disorder is a disabling condition which adversely affects a person's family, work or school life, sleeping and eating habits, and general health.
Tranquilizer	A tranquilizer, is a drug that induces tranquillity in an individual. The term "tranquilizer" is imprecise, and is usually qualified, or replaced with more precise terms: • minor tranquilizer usually refers to anxiolytic or antianxiety agent • major tranquilizer usually refers to antipsychotics

Antimanic agents can also be considered tranquilizing agents.

In music

- "Tranquilizer" is a song written by Tom Stephan ' Neil Tennant, from album Superchumbo "WowieZowie" (2005).

- Tranquilizer by Fat Jon The Ample Soul Physician, from album Repaint Tomorow

.

Ephedrine	Ephedrine is a sympathomimetic amine commonly used as a stimulant, appetite suppressant, concentration aid, decongestant, and to treat hypotension associated with anaesthesia. Ephedrine is similar in structure to the (semi-synthetic) derivatives amphetamine and methamphetamine. Chemically, it is an alkaloid derived from various plants in the genus Ephedra (family Ephedraceae). It works mainly by increasing the activity of noradrenaline on adrenergic receptors. It is most usually marketed in the hydrochloride and sulfate forms.
Alcohol Abuse	Pie abuse, as described in the DSM-IV, is a psychiatric diagnosis describing the recurring use of alcoholic beverages despite negative consequences. Alcohol abuse is sometimes referred to by the less specific term alcoholism. However, many definitions of alcoholism exist, and only some are compatible with alcohol abuse.
Clonidine	Clonidine is a medication used to treat several medical conditions. It is a direct-acting α_2 adrenergic agonist and an imidazoline. It has been prescribed historically as an antihypertensive drug. It has found new uses, including treatment of some types of neuropathic pain, opioid detoxification, sleep hyperhidrosis, anaesthetic use, and off-label, to counter the side effects of stimulant medications such as methylphenidate or amphetamine. It is becoming a more accepted treatment for insomnia, as well as for relief of menopausal symptoms.
Posttraumatic stress disorder	Posttraumatic stress disorder is a severe anxiety disorder that can develop after exposure to any event that results in psychological trauma. This event may involve the threat of death to oneself or to someone else, or to one's own or someone else's physical, sexual, or psychological integrity, overwhelming the individual's ability to cope. As an effect of psychological trauma, Posttraumatic stress disorder is less frequent and more enduring than the more commonly seen acute stress response.

Chapter 3. UPPERS

Histamine antagonist	A histamine antagonist is an agent that inhibits action of histamine via histamine receptors. H_1 antihistamines are used as treatment for symptoms of allergies, such as runny nose. Allergies are caused by an excessive type 1 hypersensitivity response of the body to allergens, such as pollen released by plants. An allergic reaction, which if severe enough can lead to anaphylaxis, results in excessive release of histamines and other mediators by the body. Other uses of H_1 antihistamines help with symptoms of local inflammation that result from various conditions, such as insect stings, even if there is no allergic reaction. Other commonly used examples of antihistamines include the H_2 antagonists (cimetidine), which are widely used for the treatment of acid reflux and stomach ulcers, as they decrease gastric acid production.
Diphenhydramine	Diphenhydramine hydrochloride is a first generation antihistamine mainly used to treat allergies. Like most other first generation antihistamines, the drug also has a powerful hypnotic effect, and for this reason is often used as a nonprescription sleep aid and a mild anxiolytic. The drug also acts as an antiemetic.
Ginseng	Ginseng is any one of eleven distinct species of slow-growing perennial plants with fleshy roots, belonging to the Panax genus in the family Araliaceae. It grows in the Northern Hemisphere in eastern Asia (mostly northern China, Korea, and eastern Siberia), typically in cooler climates; Panax vietnamensis, discovered in Vietnam, is the southernmost ginseng found quinquefolius. Ginseng is characterized by the presence of ginsenosides.
Endorphin	Endorphins ("endogenous morphine") are endogenous opioid peptides that function as neurotransmitters. They are produced by the pituitary gland and the hypothalamus in vertebrates during exercise, excitement, pain, consumption of spicy food, love and orgasm, and they resemble the opiates in their abilities to produce analgesia and a feeling of well-being. The term "endorphin" implies a pharmacological activity (analogous to the activity of the corticosteroid category of biochemicals) as opposed to a specific chemical formulation.
Insulin	Insulin is a hormone that is central to regulating carbohydrate and fat metabolism in the body. Insulin causes cells in the liver, muscle, and fat tissue to take up glucose from the blood, storing it as glycogen in the liver and muscle.

Insulin stops the use of fat as an energy source by inhibiting the release of glucagon. When insulin is absent, glucose is not taken up by body cells and the body begins to use fat as an energy source or gluconeogenesis; for example, by transfer of lipids from adipose tissue to the liver for mobilization as an energy source. As its level is a central metabolic control mechanism, its status is also used as a control signal to other body systems (such as amino acid uptake by body cells). In addition, it has several other anabolic effects throughout the body.

Desipramine

Desipramine is a tricyclic antidepressant (TCA). It inhibits the reuptake of norepinephrine and to a lesser extent serotonin. It is used to treat depression, but not considered a first line treatment since the introduction of SSRI antidepressants. Desipramine is an active metabolite of imipramine.

Chapter 4. DOWNERS: OPIATES/OPIOIDS & SEDATIVE-HYPNOTICS

DEPRESSANT	Depressants are psychoactive drugs that temporarily reduce the function or activity of a specific part of the body or brain. Examples of these kinds of effects may include anxiolysis, sedation, and hypotension. Due to their effects typically having a "down" quality to them, depressants are also occasionally referred to as "downers".
ALCOHOL	In chemistry, an alcohol is any organic compound in which a hydroxyl functional group (-OH) is bound to a carbon atom, usually connected to other carbon or hydrogen atoms. An important class are the simple acyclic alcohols, the general formula for which is $C_nH_{2n+1}OH$. Of those, ethanol (C_2H_5OH) is the type of alcohol found in alcoholic beverages, and in common speech the word alcohol refers specifically to ethanol.
BARBITURATE	Barbiturates are drugs that act as central nervous system depressants, and, by virtue of this, they produce a wide spectrum of effects, from mild sedation to total anesthesia. They are also effective as anxiolytics, as hypnotics, and as anticonvulsants. They have addiction potential, both physical and psychological. Barbiturates have now largely been replaced by benzodiazepines in routine medical practice - for example, in the treatment of anxiety and insomnia - mainly because benzodiazepines are significantly less dangerous in overdose. However, barbiturates are still used in general anesthesia, as well as for epilepsy. Barbiturates are derivatives of barbituric acid.
MDMA	MDMA - colloquially known as ecstasy, often abbreviated "E" or "X" - is an entactogenic drug of the phenethylamine and amphetamine class of drugs. MDMA can induce euphoria, a sense of intimacy with others, and diminished anxiety and depression. Many, particularly in the fields of psychology and cognitive therapy, have suggested MDMA might have therapeutic benefits and facilitate therapy sessions in certain individuals, a practice which it had formally been used for in the past.

Chapter 4. DOWNERS: OPIATES/OPIOIDS & SEDATIVE-HYPNOTICS

Histamine antagonist	A histamine antagonist is an agent that inhibits action of histamine via histamine receptors. H_1 antihistamines are used as treatment for symptoms of allergies, such as runny nose. Allergies are caused by an excessive type 1 hypersensitivity response of the body to allergens, such as pollen released by plants. An allergic reaction, which if severe enough can lead to anaphylaxis, results in excessive release of histamines and other mediators by the body. Other uses of H_1 antihistamines help with symptoms of local inflammation that result from various conditions, such as insect stings, even if there is no allergic reaction. Other commonly used examples of antihistamines include the H_2 antagonists (cimetidine), which are widely used for the treatment of acid reflux and stomach ulcers, as they decrease gastric acid production.
Carisoprodol	Carisoprodol is a centrally-acting skeletal muscle relaxant. It is a colorless, crystalline powder, having a mild characteristic odor and a bitter taste. Carisoprodol is slightly soluble in water and freely soluble in alcohol, chloroform and acetone. The drug's solubility is practically independent of pH. Carisoprodol is manufactured and marketed in the United States by Meda Pharmaceuticals Inc. under the brand name SOMA, and in the United Kingdom and other countries under the brand names Sanoma and Carisoma. The drug is available by itself or mixed with aspirin and in one preparation (Soma Compound With Codeine) along with codeine and caffeine as well.
Chloral hydrate	Chloral hydrate is a sedative and hypnotic drug as well as a chemical reagent and precursor. The name chloral hydrate indicates that it is formed from chloral (trichloroacetaldehyde) by the addition of one molecule of water. Its chemical formula is $C_2H_3Cl_3O_2$.
Cyclobenzaprine	Cyclobenzaprine is a muscle relaxant medication used to relieve skeletal muscle spasms and associated pain in acute musculoskeletal conditions. It is the most well-studied drug for this application, and it also has been used off-label for fibromyalgia treatment.
Diphenhydramine	Diphenhydramine hydrochloride is a first generation antihistamine mainly used to treat allergies. Like most other first generation antihistamines, the drug also has a powerful hypnotic effect, and for this reason is often used as a nonprescription sleep aid and a mild anxiolytic. The drug also acts as an antiemetic.
Endorphin	Endorphins ("endogenous morphine") are endogenous opioid peptides that function as neurotransmitters. They are produced by the pituitary gland and the hypothalamus in vertebrates during exercise, excitement, pain, consumption of spicy food, love and orgasm, and they resemble the opiates in their abilities to produce analgesia and a feeling of well-being.

The term "endorphin" implies a pharmacological activity (analogous to the activity of the corticosteroid category of biochemicals) as opposed to a specific chemical formulation.

Meprobamate	Meprobamate is a carbamate derivative which is used as an anxiolytic drug. It was the best-selling minor tranquilizer for a time, but has largely been replaced by the benzodiazepines.

History

Meprobamate was first synthesized by Bernard John Ludwig, PhD, and Frank Milan Berger, MD, at Carter Products in May 1950. Wallace Laboratories, a subsidiary of Carter Products, bought the license and named it Miltown after the borough of Milltown in New Jersey.

Muscle relaxant	A muscle relaxant is a drug which affects skeletal muscle function and decreases the muscle tone. It may be used to alleviate symptoms such as muscle spasms, pain, and hyperreflexia. The term "muscle relaxant" is used to refer to two major therapeutic groups: neuromuscular blockers and spasmolytics. Neuromuscular blockers act by interfering with transmission at the neuromuscular end plate and have no CNS activity. They are often used during surgical procedures and in intensive care and emergency medicine to cause paralysis. Spasmolytics, also known as "centrally-acting" muscle relaxants, are used to alleviate musculoskeletal pain and spasms and to reduce spasticity in a variety of neurological conditions. While both neuromuscular blockers and spasmolytics are often grouped together as muscle relaxants, the term is commonly used to refer to spasmolytics only.
Opium	Opium is the dried latex obtained from the opium poppy (Papaver somniferum). Opium contains up to 12% morphine, an alkaloid, which is frequently processed chemically to produce heroin for the illegal drug trade. The latex also includes codeine and non-narcotic alkaloids such as papaverine, thebaine and noscapine.
Serotonin	Serotonin is a monoamine neurotransmitter. Biochemically derived from tryptophan, serotonin is primarily found in the gastrointestinal (GI) tract, platelets, and in the central nervous system (CNS) of animals including humans. It is a well-known contributor to feelings of well-being; therefore it is also known as a "happiness hormone" despite not being a hormone.

Clam101

Chapter 4. DOWNERS: OPIATES/OPIOIDS & SEDATIVE-HYPNOTICS

Cocaine	Cocaine benzoylmethylecgonine (INN) is a crystalline tropane alkaloid that is obtained from the leaves of the coca plant. The name comes from "coca" in addition to the alkaloid suffix -ine, forming cocaine. It is a stimulant of the central nervous system, an appetite suppressant, and a topical anesthetic. Specifically, it is a serotonin-norepinephrine-dopamine reuptake inhibitor, which mediates functionality of these neurotransmitters as an exogenous catecholamine transporter ligand. Because of the way it affects the mesolimbic reward pathway, cocaine is addictive.
Morpheus	Morpheus in Greek mythology is the god of dreams, leader of the Oneiroi. Morpheus has the ability to take any human form and appear in dreams. His true semblance is that of a winged daemon, imagery shared with many of his siblings.
Codeine	Codeine (a natural isomer of methylated morphine, the other being the semi-synthetic 6-methylmorphine) is an opiate used for its analgesic, antitussive, and antidiarrheal properties. Codeine is the second-most predominant alkaloid in opium, at up to 3 percent; it is much more prevalent in the Iranian poppy (Papaver bractreatum), and codeine is extracted from this species in some places although the below-mentioned morphine methylation process is still much more common. It is considered the prototype of the weak to midrange opioids.
Morphine	Supplementary data for morphine.

Structure and properties |
| Naltrexone | Naltrexone is an opioid receptor antagonist used primarily in the management of alcohol dependence and opioid dependence. It is marketed in generic form as its hydrochloride salt, naltrexone hydrochloride, and marketed under the trade names Revia and Depade. In some countries including the United States, a once-monthly extended-release injectable formulation is marketed under the trade name Vivitrol. Also in the US, Methylnaltrexone Bromide, a closely related drug, is marketed as Relistor, for the treatment of opioid induced constipation. |
| Opioid | An opioid is a chemical that works by binding to opioid receptors, which are found principally in the central and peripheral nervous system and the gastrointestinal tract. The receptors in these organ systems mediate both the beneficial effects and the side effects of opioids. |

75

Chapter 4. DOWNERS: OPIATES/OPIOIDS & SEDATIVE-HYPNOTICS

Opioids are among the world's oldest known drugs; the use of the opium poppy for its therapeutic benefits predates recorded history.

Butorphanol	Butorphanol is a morphinan-type synthetic opioid analgesic. Brand name Stadol was recently discontinued by the manufacturer. It is now only available in its generic formulations, manufactured by Novex, Mylan, Apotex and Ben Venue Laboratories. Butorphanol is most closely structurally related to levorphanol. Butorphanol is available only as butorphanol tartrate in injectable and intranasal spray formulations.
Pethidine	Pethidine is a fast-acting opioid analgesic drug. In the United States and Canada, it is more commonly known as meperidine or by its brand name Demerol.
	Pethidine was the first synthetic opioid synthesized in 1932 as a potential anti-spasmodic agent by the chemist Otto Eislib. Its analgesic properties were first recognized by Otto Schaumann working for IG Farben, Germany.
Naloxone	Naloxone is a drug used to counter the effects of opiate overdose, for example heroin or morphine overdose. Naloxone is specifically used to counteract life-threatening depression of the central nervous system and respiratory system. Naloxone is also experimentally used in the treatment for congenital insensitivity to pain with anhidrosis (CIPA), an extremely rare disorder (1 in 125 million) that renders one unable to feel pain. It is marketed under various trademarks including Narcan, Nalone, and Narcanti, and has sometimes been mistakenly called "naltrexate." It is not to be confused with naltrexone, an opioid receptor antagonist with qualitatively different effects, used for dependence treatment rather than emergency overdose treatment.
Oxycodone	Oxycodone is an opioid analgesic medication synthesized from opium-derived thebaine. It was developed in 1916 in Germany, as one of several new semi-synthetic opioids in an attempt to improve on the existing opioids: morphine, diacetylmorphine (heroin), and codeine.
	Oxycodone oral medications are generally prescribed for the relief of moderate to severe pain. Low dosages have also been prescribed for temporary relief of diarrhea. Currently it is formulated as single ingredient products or compounded products. Some common examples of compounding are oxycodone with acetaminophen/paracetamol or NSAIDs such as ibuprofen. The formulations are available as generics but are also made under various brand names.

Chapter 4. DOWNERS: OPIATES/OPIOIDS & SEDATIVE-HYPNOTICS

Oxymorphone	Oxymorphone is a powerful semi-synthetic opioid analgesic first developed in Germany circa 1914, patented in the USA by Endo Pharmaceuticals in 1955 and introduced to the United States market in January 1959 and other countries around the same time. It differs from morphine in its effects in that it generates less euphoria, sedation, itching and other histamine effects.
	The brand name Numorphan is derived by analogy to the Nucodan name for an oxycodone product (or vice versa) as well as Paramorphan/Paramorfan for dihydromorphine and Paracodin (dihydrocodeine). The only commercially available salt of oxymorphone in most of the world at this time is the hydrochloride, which has a free base conversion ratio of 0.891.
Tramadol	Tramadol hydrochloride is a centrally acting opioid analgesic, used in treating moderate to severe pain. The drug has a wide range of applications, including treatment for restless leg syndrome and fibromyalgia. It was developed by the pharmaceutical company Grünenthal GmbH in the late 1970s.
Narcotic	The term narcotic originally referred medically to any psychoactive compound with sleep-inducing properties. In the United States of America it has since become associated with opioids, commonly morphine and heroin. The term is, today, imprecisely defined and typically has negative connotations.
Methamphetamine	Methamphetamine, methylamphetamine, N-methylamphetamine, desoxyephedrine, and colloquially as "meth" or "crystal meth", is a psychostimulant of the phenethylamine and amphetamine class of drugs. It increases alertness, concentration, energy, and in high doses, can induce euphoria, enhance self-esteem, and increase libido. Methamphetamine has high potential for abuse and addiction by activating the psychological reward system via triggering a cascading release of dopamine, norepinephrine and serotonin in the brain.
Ephedrine	Ephedrine is a sympathomimetic amine commonly used as a stimulant, appetite suppressant, concentration aid, decongestant, and to treat hypotension associated with anaesthesia.
	Ephedrine is similar in structure to the (semi-synthetic) derivatives amphetamine and methamphetamine. Chemically, it is an alkaloid derived from various plants in the genus Ephedra (family Ephedraceae). It works mainly by increasing the activity of noradrenaline on adrenergic receptors. It is most usually marketed in the hydrochloride and sulfate forms.

79

Chapter 4. DOWNERS: OPIATES/OPIOIDS & SEDATIVE-HYPNOTICS

NEUROTRANSMITTER	Neurotransmitters are endogenous chemicals which transmit signals from a neuron to a target ce across a synapse. Neurotransmitters are packaged into synaptic vesicles clustered beneath the membrane on the presynaptic side of a synapse, and are released into the synaptic cleft, where they bind to receptors in the membrane on the postsynaptic side of the synapse. Release of neurotransmitters usually follows arrival of an action potential at the synapse, but may also follov graded electrical potentials.
Salvia divinorum	Salvia divinorum is a psychoactive plant which can induce dissociative effects and is a potent producer of "visions" and other hallucinatory experiences. Its native habitat is within cloud forest in the isolated Sierra Mazateca of Oaxaca, Mexico, growing in shady and moist locations. The plant grows to over a meter high, has hollow square stems, large leaves, and occasional white flowers with violet calyx.
Brainstem	In vertebrate anatomy the brainstem is the posterior part of the brain, adjoining and structurally continuous with the spinal cord. The brain stem provides the main motor and sensory innervation to the face and neck via the cranial nerves. Though small, this is an extremely important part of the brain as the nerve connections of the motor and sensory systems from the main part of the brain to the rest of the body pass through the brain stem.
Dopamine	Dopamine is a catecholamine neurotransmitter present in a wide variety of animals, including both vertebrates and invertebrates. In the brain, this substituted phenethylamine functions as a neurotransmitter, activating the five known types of dopamine receptors--D_1, D_2, D_3, D_4, and D_5-- and their variants. Dopamine is produced in several areas of the brain, including the substantia nigra and the ventral tegmental area.
Dopaminergic	Dopaminergic means related to the neurotransmitter dopamine. For example, certain proteins such as the dopamine transporter (DAT), vesicular monoamine transporter 2 ($VMAT_2$), and dopamine receptors can be classified as dopaminergic, and neurons which synthesize or contain dopamine and synapses with dopamine receptors in them may also be labeled as dopaminergic. Enzymes which regulate the biosynthesis or metabolism of dopamine such as aromatic L-amino acid decarboxylase (AAAD) or DOPA decarboxylase (DDC), monoamine oxidase (MAO), and catechol O-methyl transferase (COMT) may be referred to as dopaminergic as well.
Nucleus accumbens	The nucleus accumbens also known as the accumbens nucleus or as the nucleus accumbens septi, is a collection of neurons within the striatum. It is thought to play an important role in reward, pleasure, laughter, addiction, aggression, fear, and the placebo effect.

	Each half of the brain has one nucleus accumbens.
Norepinephrine	Norepinephrine is a catecholamine with multiple roles including as a hormone and a neurotransmitter. As a stress hormone, norepinephrine affects parts of the brain, such as the amygdala, where attention and responses are controlled. Along with epinephrine, norepinephrine also underlies the fight-or-flight response, directly increasing heart rate, triggering the release of glucose from energy stores, and increasing blood flow to skeletal muscle. It increases the brain's oxygen supply. Norepinephrine can also suppress neuroinflammation when released diffusely in the brain from the locus ceruleus.
Cannabis	Cannabis is a genus of flowering plants that includes three putative species, Cannabis sativa, Cannabis indica, and Cannabis ruderalis. These three taxa are indigenous to Central Asia, and South Asia. Cannabis has long been used for fibre (hemp), for seed and seed oils, for medicinal purposes, and as a recreational drug.
Substance abuse	Substance abuse refers to a maladaptive pattern of use of a substance that is not considered dependent. The term "drug abuse" does not exclude dependency, but is otherwise used in a similar manner in nonmedical contexts. The terms have a huge range of definitions related to taking a psychoactive drug or performance enhancing drug for a non-therapeutic or non-medical effect.
Hallucinogen persisting perception disorder	Hallucinogen persisting perception disorder are reminiscent of those generated by the ingestion of hallucinogenic substances. Previous use of hallucinogens by the person is needed, though not sufficient, for diagnosing someone with the disorder. For an individual to be diagnosed with Hallucinogen persisting perception disorder, the symptoms cannot be due to another medical condition.
Perception	In philosophy, psychology, and cognitive science, perception is the process of attaining awareness or understanding of sensory information. The word "perception" comes from the Latin words perceptio, percipio, and means "receiving, collecting, action of taking possession, apprehension with the mind or senses."

	Perception is one of the oldest fields in psychology. The oldest quantitative law in psychology is the Weber-Fechner law, which quantifies the relationship between the intensity of physical stimuli and their perceptual effects.
Stimulant	Stimulants are psychoactive drugs which induce temporary improvements in either mental or physical function or both. Examples of these kinds of effects may include enhanced alertness, wakefulness, and locomotion, among others. Due to their effects typically having an "up" quality to them, stimulants are also occasionally referred to as "uppers".
Speedball	Speedball is a term commonly referring to the hazardous intravenous use of heroin and cocaine together in the same syringe. Cocaine acts as a stimulant, whereas heroin acts as a depressant. Coadministration provides an intense rush of euphoria with a high that combines both effects of the drugs, while excluding the negative effects, such as anxiety and sedation.
Clonazepam	Clonazepam is a benzodiazepine derivative with anticonvulsant, muscle relaxant, and very potent anxiolytic properties. It is marketed by Roche under the trade-names Klonopin in the United States, and Ravotril in Chile. Other names like Rivotril or Rivatril are known throughout the large majority of the rest of the world. Clonazepam has an unusually long half-life of 18-50 hours, making it generally considered to be among the long-acting benzodiazepines. Clonazepam is a chlorinated derivative of nitrazepam and therefore a nitrobenzodiazepine.
Clonidine	Clonidine is a medication used to treat several medical conditions. It is a direct-acting α_2 adrenergic agonist and an imidazoline. It has been prescribed historically as an antihypertensive drug. It has found new uses, including treatment of some types of neuropathic pain, opioid detoxification, sleep hyperhidrosis, anaesthetic use, and off-label, to counter the side effects of stimulant medications such as methylphenidate or amphetamine. It is becoming a more accepted treatment for insomnia, as well as for relief of menopausal symptoms.
Desipramine	Desipramine is a tricyclic antidepressant (TCA). It inhibits the reuptake of norepinephrine and to a lesser extent serotonin. It is used to treat depression, but not considered a first line treatment since the introduction of SSRI antidepressants. Desipramine is an active metabolite of imipramine.

85

Chapter 4. DOWNERS: OPIATES/OPIOIDS & SEDATIVE-HYPNOTICS

Butabarbital	Butabarbital is a prescription barbiturate sleep aid. Butabarbital has a particularly fast onset of effects and short duration of action compared to other barbiturates, which makes it useful for certain applications such as treating severe insomnia and relieving anxiety before surgical procedures; however it is also relatively dangerous particularly when combined with alcohol, and so is now rarely used, although it is still prescribed in some Eastern European and South American countries. Its intermediate duration of action gives butabarbital an abuse potential slightly lower than secobarbital.
Chlordiazepoxide	Chlordiazepoxide, is a sedative/hypnotic drug and benzodiazepine derivative. It is marketed under the trade names Klopoxid, Librax (also contains clidinium bromide), Libritabs, Librium, Mesural, Multum, Novapam, Risolid, Silibrin, Sonimen, Tropium, and Zetran.
	Chlordiazepoxide was the first benzodiazepine to be synthesised and the discovery of chlordiazepoxide was by pure chance. Chlordiazepoxide and other benzodiazepines were initially accepted with widespread public approval but were followed with widespread public disapproval and recommendations for more restrictive medical guidelines for its use.
Flurazepam	Flurazepam is a drug which is a benzodiazepine derivative. It possesses anxiolytic, anticonvulsant, sedative and skeletal muscle relaxant properties. It produces a metabolite with a very long half-life (40-250 hours), which may stay in the bloodstream for up to four days.
Glutethimide	Glutethimide is a hypnotic sedative that was introduced in 1954 as a safe alternative to barbiturates to treat insomnia. Before long, however, it had become clear that glutethimide was just as likely to cause addiction and caused similarly severe withdrawal symptoms. Doriden is the brand-name version of the drug; both the generic and brand-name forms are rarely prescribed today.
Methaqualone	Methaqualone is a sedative-hypnotic drug that is similar in effect to barbiturates, a general central nervous system depressant. Its use peaked in the 1960s and 1970s as a hypnotic, for the treatment of insomnia, and as a sedative and muscle relaxant. It has also been used illegally as a recreational drug, commonly known as Quaaludes, Sopors, Ludes or Mandrax (particularly in the 1970s in North America/Canada) depending on the manufacturer.
Oxazepam	Oxazepam is a drug which is a benzodiazepine derivative. Oxazepam is a benzodiazepine used extensively since the 1960s for the treatment of anxiety and insomnia and in the control of symptoms of alcohol withdrawal. It is a metabolite of diazepam, prazepam and temazepam. Oxazepam has moderate amnesic, anxiolytic, anticonvulsant, hypnotic, sedative and skeletal muscle relaxant properties compared to other benzodiazepines.

Chapter 4. DOWNERS: OPIATES/OPIOIDS & SEDATIVE-HYPNOTICS

Paraldehyde	Paraldehyde is the cyclic trimer of acetaldehyde molecules. Formally, it is a derivative of 1,3,5-trioxane. The corresponding tetramer is metaldehyde. A colourless liquid, it is sparingly soluble in water and highly soluble in alcohol. Paraldehyde slowly oxidizes in air, turning brown and producing an odor of acetic acid. It quickly reacts with most plastics and rubber.
Pentobarbital	Pentobarbital is a short-acting barbiturate that was first synthesized in 1928. Pentobarbital is available as both a free acid and a sodium salt, the former of which is only slightly soluble in water and ethanol. One trade name for this drug is Nembutal, coined by Dr. John S. Lundy, who started using it in 1930, from the structural formula of the sodium salt--Na (sodium) + ethyl + methyl + butyl + al (common suffix for barbiturates).
Quazepam	Quazepam is a drug which is a benzodiazepine derivative. Quazepam is indicated for the treatment of insomnia including sleep induction and sleep maintenance. Quazepam induces impairment of motor function and has hypnotic and anticonvulsant properties with less overdose potential than other benzodiazepines.
Sodium thiopental	Sodium thiopental is a rapid-onset short-acting barbiturate general anaesthetic. Thiopental is a core medicine in the World Health Organization's "Essential Drugs List", which is a list of minimum medical needs for a basic healthcare system.
Triazolam	Triazolam is a benzodiazepine derivative drug. It possesses pharmacological properties similar to that of other benzodiazepines, but it is generally only used as a sedative to treat severe insomnia. In addition to the hypnotic properties triazolam possesses, amnesic, anxiolytic, sedative, anticonvulsant and muscle relaxant properties are also present. Due to its short half-life, triazolam is not effective for patients that suffer from frequent awakenings or early wakening.
Beta blocker	Beta blockers are a class of drugs used for various indications, but particularly for the management of cardiac arrhythmias, cardioprotection after myocardial infarction (heart attack), and hypertension. As beta adrenergic receptor antagonists, they diminish the effects of epinephrine (adrenaline) and other stress hormones. In 1958 the first beta blocker, dichloroisoproterenol, was synthesised by Eli Lilly Laboratories, but it was Sir James W. Black in 1962, who found the first clinically significant use of beta blockers with propranolol and pronethalol; it revolutionized the medical management of angina pectoris and is considered by many to be one of the most important contributions to clinical medicine and pharmacology of the 20th century.

Fluoxetine	Fluoxetine is an antidepressant of the selective serotonin reuptake inhibitor (SSRI) class. It is manufactured and marketed by Eli Lilly and Company. In combination with olanzapine it is known as symbyax. Fluoxetine is approved for the treatment of major depression (including pediatric depression), obsessive-compulsive disorder (in both adult and pediatric populations), bulimia nervosa, panic disorder and premenstrual dysphoric disorder.
Hypnotic	Hypnotic drugs are a class of psychoactives whose primary function is to induce sleep and to be used in the treatment of insomnia and in surgical anesthesia. When used in anesthesia to produce and maintain unconsciousness, "sleep" is metaphorical and there are no regular sleep stages or cyclical natural states; patients rarely recover from anesthesia feeling refreshed and with renewed energy. Because drugs in this class generally produce dose-dependent effects, ranging from anxiolysis to production of unconsciousness, they are often referred to collectively as sedative-hypnotic drugs.
Sedative	A sedative is a substance that induces sedation by reducing irritability or excitement. At higher doses it may result in slurred speech, staggering gait, poor judgment, and slow, uncertain reflexes. Doses of sedatives such as benzodiazepines when used as a hypnotic to induce sleep tend to be higher than those used to relieve anxiety whereas only low doses are needed to provide calming sedative effects.
Tranquilizer	A tranquilizer, is a drug that induces tranquillity in an individual. The term "tranquilizer" is imprecise, and is usually qualified, or replaced with more precise terms: • minor tranquilizer usually refers to anxiolytic or antianxiety agent • major tranquilizer usually refers to antipsychotics

91

Antimanic agents can also be considered tranquilizing agents.

In music

- "Tranquilizer" is a song written by Tom Stephan ' Neil Tennant, from album Superchumbo "WowieZowie" (2005).

- Tranquilizer by Fat Jon The Ample Soul Physician, from album Repaint Tomorow

.

Antipsychotic	An antipsychotic is a tranquilizing psychiatric medication primarily used to manage psychosis (including delusions or hallucinations, as well as disordered thought), particularly in schizophrenia and bipolar disorder. A first generation of antipsychotics, known as typical antipsychotics, was discovered in the 1950s. Most of the drugs in the second generation, known as atypical antipsychotics, have been developed more recently, although the first atypical antipsychotic, clozapine, was discovered in the 1950s and introduced clinically in the 1970s.
Ketamine	Ketamine is a drug used in human and veterinary medicine. Its hydrochloride salt is sold as Ketanest, Ketaset, and Ketalar. Pharmacologically, ketamine is classified as an NMDA receptor antagonist.
Trazodone	Trazodone is an antidepressant of the serotonin antagonist and reuptake inhibitor (SARI) class. It is a phenylpiperazine compound. Trazodone also has anxiolytic, and hypnotic effects. Trazodone has considerably less prominent anticholinergic (dry mouth, constipation, tachycardia) and sexual side effects than most of the tricyclic antidepressants (TCAs).
Ethanol	Ethanol, pure alcohol, grain alcohol, or drinking alcohol, is a volatile, flammable, colorless liquid. It is a powerful psychoactive drug and one of the oldest recreational drugs. Best known as the type of alcohol found in alcoholic beverages, it is also used in thermometers, as a solvent, and as an alcohol fuel.
Narcolepsy	Narcolepsy is a chronic sleep disorder, or dyssomnia, characterized by excessive daytime sleepiness (EDS) in which a person experiences extreme fatigue and possibly falls asleep at inappropriate times, such as while at work or at school. Narcoleptics usually experience disturbed nocturnal sleep and an abnormal daytime sleep pattern, which is often confused with insomnia. When a narcoleptic falls asleep they generally experience the REM stage of sleep within 10 minutes; whereas most people do not experience REM sleep until after 90 minutes.

Interaction

In medicine, most medications can be safely used with other medicines, but particular combinations of medicines need to be monitored for interactions, often by the pharmacist. Interactions between medications (drug interactions) fall generally into one of two main categories:

1. pharmacodynamic : Involving the actions of the two interacting drugs.
2. pharmacokinetic : Involving the absorption, distribution, metabolism, and excretion of one or both of the interacting drugs upon the other.

Chapter 5. DOWNERS: ALCOHOL

ALCOHOL	In chemistry, an alcohol is any organic compound in which a hydroxyl functional group (-OH) is bound to a carbon atom, usually connected to other carbon or hydrogen atoms.
	An important class are the simple acyclic alcohols, the general formula for which is $C_nH_{2n+1}OH$. Of those, ethanol (C_2H_5OH) is the type of alcohol found in alcoholic beverages, and in common speech the word alcohol refers specifically to ethanol.
MDMA	MDMA - colloquially known as ecstasy, often abbreviated "E" or "X" - is an entactogenic drug of the phenethylamine and amphetamine class of drugs.
	MDMA can induce euphoria, a sense of intimacy with others, and diminished anxiety and depression. Many, particularly in the fields of psychology and cognitive therapy, have suggested MDMA might have therapeutic benefits and facilitate therapy sessions in certain individuals, a practice which it had formally been used for in the past.
Alcoholic beverage	An alcoholic beverage is a drink containing ethanol, commonly known as alcohol. Alcoholic beverages are divided into three general classes: beers, wines, and spirits. They are legally consumed in most countries, and over 100 countries have laws regulating their production, sale, and consumption.
Brainstem	In vertebrate anatomy the brainstem is the posterior part of the brain, adjoining and structurally continuous with the spinal cord. The brain stem provides the main motor and sensory innervation to the face and neck via the cranial nerves. Though small, this is an extremely important part of the brain as the nerve connections of the motor and sensory systems from the main part of the brain to the rest of the body pass through the brain stem.
Ethanol	Ethanol, pure alcohol, grain alcohol, or drinking alcohol, is a volatile, flammable, colorless liquid. It is a powerful psychoactive drug and one of the oldest recreational drugs. Best known as the type of alcohol found in alcoholic beverages, it is also used in thermometers, as a solvent, and as an alcohol fuel.
Ketamine	Ketamine is a drug used in human and veterinary medicine. Its hydrochloride salt is sold as Ketanest, Ketaset, and Ketalar. Pharmacologically, ketamine is classified as an NMDA receptor antagonist.

Chapter 5. DOWNERS: ALCOHOL

BARBITURATE	Barbiturates are drugs that act as central nervous system depressants, and, by virtue of this, they produce a wide spectrum of effects, from mild sedation to total anesthesia. They are also effective as anxiolytics, as hypnotics, and as anticonvulsants. They have addiction potential, both physical and psychological. Barbiturates have now largely been replaced by benzodiazepines in routine medical practice - for example, in the treatment of anxiety and insomnia - mainly because benzodiazepines are significantly less dangerous in overdose. However, barbiturates are still used in general anesthesia, as well as for epilepsy. Barbiturates are derivatives of barbituric acid.
Acetaldehyde	Acetaldehyde is an organic chemical compound with the formula CH_3CHO or MeCHO. It is one of the most important aldehydes, occurring widely in nature and being produced on a large scale industrially. Acetaldehyde occurs naturally in coffee, bread, and ripe fruit, and is produced by plants as part of their normal metabolism. It is also produced by oxidation of ethanol and is popularly believed to be a cause of hangovers. Pathways of exposure include air, water, land or groundwater that can expose the human subject directly if they inhale, drink, or smoke.
Desipramine	Desipramine is a tricyclic antidepressant (TCA). It inhibits the reuptake of norepinephrine and to a lesser extent serotonin. It is used to treat depression, but not considered a first line treatment since the introduction of SSRI antidepressants. Desipramine is an active metabolite of imipramine.
Estrogen	Estrogens (AmE), oestrogens (BE), or œstrogens, are a group of compounds named for their importance in the estrous cycle of humans and other animals, and functioning as the primary female sex hormones. Natural estrogens are steroid hormones, while some synthetic ones are non-steroidal.
NEUROTRANSMITTER	Neurotransmitters are endogenous chemicals which transmit signals from a neuron to a target ce across a synapse. Neurotransmitters are packaged into synaptic vesicles clustered beneath the membrane on the presynaptic side of a synapse, and are released into the synaptic cleft, where they bind to receptors in the membrane on the postsynaptic side of the synapse. Release of neurotransmitters usually follows arrival of an action potential at the synapse, but may also follov graded electrical potentials.
Dopamine	Dopamine is a catecholamine neurotransmitter present in a wide variety of animals, including both vertebrates and invertebrates. In the brain, this substituted phenethylamine functions as a neurotransmitter, activating the five known types of dopamine receptors--D_1, D_2, D_3, D_4, and D_5-- and their variants. Dopamine is produced in several areas of the brain, including the substantia nigra and the ventral tegmental area.

Chapter 5. DOWNERS: ALCOHOL

Dopaminergic	Dopaminergic means related to the neurotransmitter dopamine. For example, certain proteins such as the dopamine transporter (DAT), vesicular monoamine transporter 2 ($VMAT_2$), and dopamine receptors can be classified as dopaminergic, and neurons which synthesize or contain dopamine and synapses with dopamine receptors in them may also be labeled as dopaminergic. Enzymes which regulate the biosynthesis or metabolism of dopamine such as aromatic L-amino acid decarboxylase (AAAD) or DOPA decarboxylase (DDC), monoamine oxidase (MAO), and catechol O-methyl transferase (COMT) may be referred to as dopaminergic as well.
Limbic system	The limbic system is a set of brain structures including the hippocampus, amygdala, anterior thalamic nuclei, septum, limbic cortex and fornix, which seemingly support a variety of functions including emotion, behavior, long term memory, and olfaction. The term "limbic" comes from the Latin limbus, for "border" or "edge". Some scientists have suggested that the concept of the limbic system should be abandoned as obsolete, as it is grounded more in transient tradition than in facts.
Norepinephrine	Norepinephrine is a catecholamine with multiple roles including as a hormone and a neurotransmitter.
	As a stress hormone, norepinephrine affects parts of the brain, such as the amygdala, where attention and responses are controlled. Along with epinephrine, norepinephrine also underlies the fight-or-flight response, directly increasing heart rate, triggering the release of glucose from energy stores, and increasing blood flow to skeletal muscle. It increases the brain's oxygen supply. Norepinephrine can also suppress neuroinflammation when released diffusely in the brain from the locus ceruleus.
Stimulant	Stimulants are psychoactive drugs which induce temporary improvements in either mental or physical function or both. Examples of these kinds of effects may include enhanced alertness, wakefulness, and locomotion, among others. Due to their effects typically having an "up" quality to them, stimulants are also occasionally referred to as "uppers".
Salvia divinorum	Salvia divinorum is a psychoactive plant which can induce dissociative effects and is a potent producer of "visions" and other hallucinatory experiences. Its native habitat is within cloud forest in the isolated Sierra Mazateca of Oaxaca, Mexico, growing in shady and moist locations. The plant grows to over a meter high, has hollow square stems, large leaves, and occasional white flowers with violet calyx.

Chapter 5. DOWNERS: ALCOHOL

Antipsychotic	An antipsychotic is a tranquilizing psychiatric medication primarily used to manage psychosis (including delusions or hallucinations, as well as disordered thought), particularly in schizophrenia and bipolar disorder. A first generation of antipsychotics, known as typical antipsychotics, was discovered in the 1950s. Most of the drugs in the second generation, known as atypical antipsychotics, have been developed more recently, although the first atypical antipsychotic, clozapine, was discovered in the 1950s and introduced clinically in the 1970s.
Anxiety disorder	Anxiety disorders are blanket terms covering several different forms of abnormal and pathological fear and anxiety which only came under the aegis of psychiatry at the very end of the 19th century. Gelder, Mayou ' Geddes (2005) explains that anxiety disorders are classified in two groups: continuous symptoms and episodic symptoms. Current psychiatric diagnostic criteria recognize a wide variety of anxiety disorders.
Opioid	An opioid is a chemical that works by binding to opioid receptors, which are found principally in the central and peripheral nervous system and the gastrointestinal tract. The receptors in these organ systems mediate both the beneficial effects and the side effects of opioids. Opioids are among the world's oldest known drugs; the use of the opium poppy for its therapeutic benefits predates recorded history.
Cannabis	Cannabis is a genus of flowering plants that includes three putative species, Cannabis sativa, Cannabis indica, and Cannabis ruderalis. These three taxa are indigenous to Central Asia, and South Asia. Cannabis has long been used for fibre (hemp), for seed and seed oils, for medicinal purposes, and as a recreational drug.
Substance abuse	Substance abuse refers to a maladaptive pattern of use of a substance that is not considered dependent. The term "drug abuse" does not exclude dependency, but is otherwise used in a similar manner in nonmedical contexts. The terms have a huge range of definitions related to taking a psychoactive drug or performance enhancing drug for a non-therapeutic or non-medical effect.
Dementia	Dementia is a serious loss of cognitive ability in a previously unimpaired person, beyond what might be expected from normal aging. It may be static, the result of a unique global brain injury, or progressive, resulting in long-term decline due to damage or disease in the body. Although dementia is far more common in the geriatric population, it may occur in any stage of adulthood.

Chapter 5. DOWNERS: ALCOHOL

Depressant	Depressants are psychoactive drugs that temporarily reduce the function or activity of a specific part of the body or brain. Examples of these kinds of effects may include anxiolysis, sedation, and hypotension. Due to their effects typically having a "down" quality to them, depressants are also occasionally referred to as "downers".
Hypoglycemia	Hypoglycemia is the medical term for a state produced by a lower than normal level of blood glucose. The term literally means "under-sweet blood" . It can produce a variety of symptoms and effects but the principal problems arise from an inadequate supply of glucose to the brain, resulting in impairment of function (neuroglycopenia).
Insulin	Insulin is a hormone that is central to regulating carbohydrate and fat metabolism in the body. Insulin causes cells in the liver, muscle, and fat tissue to take up glucose from the blood, storing it as glycogen in the liver and muscle.
	Insulin stops the use of fat as an energy source by inhibiting the release of glucagon. When insulin is absent, glucose is not taken up by body cells and the body begins to use fat as an energy source or gluconeogenesis; for example, by transfer of lipids from adipose tissue to the liver for mobilization as an energy source. As its level is a central metabolic control mechanism, its status is also used as a control signal to other body systems (such as amino acid uptake by body cells). In addition, it has several other anabolic effects throughout the body.
Serotonin	Serotonin is a monoamine neurotransmitter. Biochemically derived from tryptophan, serotonin is primarily found in the gastrointestinal (GI) tract, platelets, and in the central nervous system (CNS) of animals including humans. It is a well-known contributor to feelings of well-being; therefore it is also known as a "happiness hormone" despite not being a hormone.
Nucleus accumbens	The nucleus accumbens also known as the accumbens nucleus or as the nucleus accumbens septi, is a collection of neurons within the striatum. It is thought to play an important role in reward, pleasure, laughter, addiction, aggression, fear, and the placebo effect.
	Each half of the brain has one nucleus accumbens.

Chapter 5. DOWNERS: ALCOHOL

Alcohol TOLERANCE	Alcohol tolerance refers to the bodily responses to the functional effects of ethanol in alcoholic beverages. This includes direct tolerance, speed of recovery from insobriety and resistance to the development of alcoholism. Consumption-induced tolerance Alcohol tolerance is increased by regular drinking.
Hallucination	A hallucination, in the broadest sense of the word, is a perception in the absence of a stimulus. In a stricter sense, hallucinations are defined as perceptions in a conscious and awake state in the absence of external stimuli which have qualities of real perception, in that they are vivid, substantial, and located in external objective space. The latter definition distinguishes hallucinations from the related phenomena of dreaming, which does not involve wakefulness; illusion, which involves distorted or misinterpreted real perception; imagery, which does not mimic real perception and is under voluntary control; and pseudohallucination, which does not mimic real perception, but is not under voluntary control.
Depression	Depression, one of the most commonly diagnosed psychiatric disorders, is being diagnosed in increasing numbers in various segments of the population worldwide. Depression in the United States alone affects 17.6 million Americans each year or 1 in 6 people. Depressed patients are at increased risk of type 2 diabetes, cardiovascular disease and suicide. Within the next twenty years depression is expected to become the second leading cause of disability worldwide and the leading cause in high-income nations, including the United States. In approximately 75% of completed suicides the individuals had seen a physician within the prior year before their death, 45%-66% within the prior month. Approximately 33% - 41% of those who completed suicide had contact with mental health services in the prior year, 20% within the prior month.
Opium	Opium is the dried latex obtained from the opium poppy (Papaver somniferum). Opium contains up to 12% morphine, an alkaloid, which is frequently processed chemically to produce heroin for the illegal drug trade. The latex also includes codeine and non-narcotic alkaloids such as papaverine, thebaine and noscapine.
Learning	Learning is acquiring new or modifying existing knowledge, behaviors, skills, values, or preferences and may involve synthesizing different types of information. The ability to learn is possessed by humans, animals and some machines. Progress over time tends to follow learning curves.

Chapter 6. ALL AROUNDERS

Cannabis	Cannabis is a genus of flowering plants that includes three putative species, Cannabis sativa, Cannabis indica, and Cannabis ruderalis. These three taxa are indigenous to Central Asia, and South Asia. Cannabis has long been used for fibre (hemp), for seed and seed oils, for medicinal purposes, and as a recreational drug.
MDMA	MDMA - colloquially known as ecstasy, often abbreviated "E" or "X" - is an entactogenic drug of the phenethylamine and amphetamine class of drugs. MDMA can induce euphoria, a sense of intimacy with others, and diminished anxiety and depression. Many, particularly in the fields of psychology and cognitive therapy, have suggested MDMA might have therapeutic benefits and facilitate therapy sessions in certain individuals, a practice which it had formally been used for in the past.
Salvia divinorum	Salvia divinorum is a psychoactive plant which can induce dissociative effects and is a potent producer of "visions" and other hallucinatory experiences. Its native habitat is within cloud forest in the isolated Sierra Mazateca of Oaxaca, Mexico, growing in shady and moist locations. The plant grows to over a meter high, has hollow square stems, large leaves, and occasional white flowers with violet calyx.
Benzatropine	Benzatropine is an anticholinergic marketed under the trade name Cogentin which is used in the treatment of Parkinson's disease, parkinsonism, akathisia, and dystonia. Benzatropine is used in patients to reduce the side effects of antipsychotic treatment, such as parkinsonism and akathisia. Benzatropine is also a second-line drug for the treatment of Parkinson's disease.
Psychoactive drug	A psychoactive drug, psychopharmaceutical, or psychotropic is a chemical substance that crosses the blood-brain barrier and acts primarily upon the central nervous system where it affects brain function, resulting in changes in perception, mood, consciousness, cognition, and behavior. These substances may be used recreationally, to purposefully alter one's consciousness, as entheogens, for ritual, spiritual, and/or shamanic purposes, as a tool for studying or augmenting the mind, or therapeutically as medication.

Chapter 6. ALL AROUNDERS

Because psychoactive substances bring about subjective changes in consciousness and mood that the user may find pleasant (e.g. euphoria) or advantageous (e.g. increased alertness), many psychoactive substances are abused, that is, used excessively, despite the health risks or negative consequences.

Methamphetamine

Methamphetamine, methylamphetamine, N-methylamphetamine, desoxyephedrine, and colloquially as "meth" or "crystal meth", is a psychostimulant of the phenethylamine and amphetamine class of drugs. It increases alertness, concentration, energy, and in high doses, can induce euphoria, enhance self-esteem, and increase libido. Methamphetamine has high potential for abuse and addiction by activating the psychological reward system via triggering a cascading release of dopamine, norepinephrine and serotonin in the brain.

Phencyclidine

Phencyclidine (a complex clip of the chemical name 1-(1-phenylcyclohexyl)piperidine, commonly initialized as PCP), also known as angel dust and myriad other street names, is a recreational, dissociative drug formerly used as an anesthetic agent, exhibiting hallucinogenic and neurotoxic effects.

Developed in 1926, it was first patented in 1952 by the Parke-Davis pharmaceutical company and marketed under the brand name Sernyl. In chemical structure, PCP is an arylcyclohexylamine derivative, and, in pharmacology, it is a member of the family of dissociative anesthetics. PCP works primarily as an NMDA receptor antagonist, which blocks the activity of the NMDA receptor and, like most antiglutamatergic hallucinogens, is significantly more dangerous than other categories of hallucinogens. Other NMDA receptor antagonists include ketamine, tiletamine, and dextromethorphan. Although the primary psychoactive effects of the drug lasts for a few hours, the total elimination rate from the body typically extends eight days or longer.

Anticholinergic

An anticholinergic agent is a substance that blocks the neurotransmitter acetylcholine in the central and the peripheral nervous system. An example of an anticholinergic is dicycloverine, and the classic example is atropine. Anticholinergics are administered to reduce the effects mediated by acetylcholine on acetylcholine receptors in neurons through competitive inhibition. Therefore, their effects are reversible.

Ibogaine

Ibogaine is a naturally occurring psychoactive substance found in a number of plants, principally in a member of the Apocynaceae family known as iboga (Tabernanthe iboga).

Chapter 6. ALL AROUNDERS

A hallucinogen, the substance is banned in some countries; in other countries it is being used to treat addiction to opiates, methamphetamine and other drugs. Derivatives of ibogaine that lack the substance's hallucinogen properties are under development.

Ketamine

Ketamine is a drug used in human and veterinary medicine. Its hydrochloride salt is sold as Ketanest, Ketaset, and Ketalar. Pharmacologically, ketamine is classified as an NMDA receptor antagonist.

Khat

Khat is a flowering plant native to tropical East Africa and the Arabian Peninsula.

Khat contains the alkaloid called cathinone, an amphetamine-like stimulant which is said to cause excitement, loss of appetite, and euphoria. In 1980, the World Health Organization classified khat as a drug of abuse that can produce mild to moderate psychological dependence (less than tobacco or alcohol). The plant has been targeted by anti-drug organizations like the DEA. It is a controlled or illegal substance in many countries, but is legal for sale and production in many others.

Alcohol

In chemistry, an alcohol is any organic compound in which a hydroxyl functional group (-OH) is bound to a carbon atom, usually connected to other carbon or hydrogen atoms.

An important class are the simple acyclic alcohols, the general formula for which is $C_nH_{2n+1}OH$. Of those, ethanol (C_2H_5OH) is the type of alcohol found in alcoholic beverages, and in common speech the word alcohol refers specifically to ethanol.

Brainstem

In vertebrate anatomy the brainstem is the posterior part of the brain, adjoining and structurally continuous with the spinal cord. The brain stem provides the main motor and sensory innervation to the face and neck via the cranial nerves. Though small, this is an extremely important part of the brain as the nerve connections of the motor and sensory systems from the main part of the brain to the rest of the body pass through the brain stem.

Chapter 6. ALL AROUNDERS

Hallucination	A hallucination, in the broadest sense of the word, is a perception in the absence of a stimulus. In a stricter sense, hallucinations are defined as perceptions in a conscious and awake state in the absence of external stimuli which have qualities of real perception, in that they are vivid, substantial, and located in external objective space. The latter definition distinguishes hallucinations from the related phenomena of dreaming, which does not involve wakefulness; illusion, which involves distorted or misinterpreted real perception; imagery, which does not mimic real perception and is under voluntary control; and pseudohallucination, which does not mimic real perception, but is not under voluntary control.
Limbic system	The limbic system is a set of brain structures including the hippocampus, amygdala, anterior thalamic nuclei, septum, limbic cortex and fornix, which seemingly support a variety of functions including emotion, behavior, long term memory, and olfaction. The term "limbic" comes from the Latin limbus, for "border" or "edge". Some scientists have suggested that the concept of the limbic system should be abandoned as obsolete, as it is grounded more in transient tradition than in facts.
Serotonin	Serotonin is a monoamine neurotransmitter. Biochemically derived from tryptophan, serotonin is primarily found in the gastrointestinal (GI) tract, platelets, and in the central nervous system (CNS) of animals including humans. It is a well-known contributor to feelings of well-being; therefore it is also known as a "happiness hormone" despite not being a hormone.
BARBITURATE	Barbiturates are drugs that act as central nervous system depressants, and, by virtue of this, they produce a wide spectrum of effects, from mild sedation to total anesthesia. They are also effective as anxiolytics, as hypnotics, and as anticonvulsants. They have addiction potential, both physical and psychological. Barbiturates have now largely been replaced by benzodiazepines in routine medical practice - for example, in the treatment of anxiety and insomnia - mainly because benzodiazepines are significantly less dangerous in overdose. However, barbiturates are still used in general anesthesia, as well as for epilepsy. Barbiturates are derivatives of barbituric acid.
Neurotransmitter	Neurotransmitters are endogenous chemicals which transmit signals from a neuron to a target cell across a synapse. Neurotransmitters are packaged into synaptic vesicles clustered beneath the membrane on the presynaptic side of a synapse, and are released into the synaptic cleft, where they bind to receptors in the membrane on the postsynaptic side of the synapse. Release of neurotransmitters usually follows arrival of an action potential at the synapse, but may also follow graded electrical potentials.

Chapter 6. ALL AROUNDERS

Kava	Kava is a crop of the western Pacific. The roots of the plant are used to produce a drink with mild sedative properties. Kava is consumed throughout the Pacific Ocean cultures of Polynesia (including Hawaii), Vanuatu, Melanesia and some parts of Micronesia. Kava is sedating and is primarily consumed to relax without disrupting mental clarity. Its active ingredients are called kavalactones.
Opium	Opium is the dried latex obtained from the opium poppy (Papaver somniferum). Opium contains up to 12% morphine, an alkaloid, which is frequently processed chemically to produce heroin for the illegal drug trade. The latex also includes codeine and non-narcotic alkaloids such as papaverine, thebaine and noscapine.
Cocaine	Cocaine benzoylmethylecgonine (INN) is a crystalline tropane alkaloid that is obtained from the leaves of the coca plant. The name comes from "coca" in addition to the alkaloid suffix -ine, forming cocaine. It is a stimulant of the central nervous system, an appetite suppressant, and a topical anesthetic. Specifically, it is a serotonin-norepinephrine-dopamine reuptake inhibitor, which mediates functionality of these neurotransmitters as an exogenous catecholamine transporter ligand. Because of the way it affects the mesolimbic reward pathway, cocaine is addictive.
Codeine	Codeine (a natural isomer of methylated morphine, the other being the semi-synthetic 6-methylmorphine) is an opiate used for its analgesic, antitussive, and antidiarrheal properties. Codeine is the second-most predominant alkaloid in opium, at up to 3 percent; it is much more prevalent in the Iranian poppy (Papaver bractreatum), and codeine is extracted from this species in some places although the below-mentioned morphine methylation process is still much more common. It is considered the prototype of the weak to midrange opioids.
Fluoxetine	Fluoxetine is an antidepressant of the selective serotonin reuptake inhibitor (SSRI) class. It is manufactured and marketed by Eli Lilly and Company. In combination with olanzapine it is known as symbyax. Fluoxetine is approved for the treatment of major depression (including pediatric depression), obsessive-compulsive disorder (in both adult and pediatric populations), bulimia nervosa, panic disorder and premenstrual dysphoric disorder.
Oxycodone	Oxycodone is an opioid analgesic medication synthesized from opium-derived thebaine. It was developed in 1916 in Germany, as one of several new semi-synthetic opioids in an attempt to improve on the existing opioids: morphine, diacetylmorphine (heroin), and codeine.

Chapter 6. ALL AROUNDERS

Oxycodone oral medications are generally prescribed for the relief of moderate to severe pain. Low dosages have also been prescribed for temporary relief of diarrhea. Currently it is formulated as single ingredient products or compounded products. Some common examples of compounding are oxycodone with acetaminophen/paracetamol or NSAIDs such as ibuprofen. The formulations are available as generics but are also made under various brand names.

Speedball

Speedball is a term commonly referring to the hazardous intravenous use of heroin and cocaine together in the same syringe.

Cocaine acts as a stimulant, whereas heroin acts as a depressant. Coadministration provides an intense rush of euphoria with a high that combines both effects of the drugs, while excluding the negative effects, such as anxiety and sedation.

Acetylcholine

The chemical compound acetylcholine is a neurotransmitter in both the peripheral nervous system (PNS) and central nervous system (CNS) in many organisms including humans. Acetylcholine is one of many neurotransmitters in the autonomic nervous system (ANS) and the only neurotransmitter used in the motor division of the somatic nervous system. (Sensory neurons use glutamate and various peptides at their synapses). Acetylcholine is also the principal neurotransmitter in all autonomic ganglia.

Dopamine

Dopamine is a catecholamine neurotransmitter present in a wide variety of animals, including both vertebrates and invertebrates. In the brain, this substituted phenethylamine functions as a neurotransmitter, activating the five known types of dopamine receptors--D_1, D_2, D_3, D_4, and D_5-- and their variants. Dopamine is produced in several areas of the brain, including the substantia nigra and the ventral tegmental area.

Endorphin

Endorphins ("endogenous morphine") are endogenous opioid peptides that function as neurotransmitters. They are produced by the pituitary gland and the hypothalamus in vertebrates during exercise, excitement, pain, consumption of spicy food, love and orgasm, and they resemble the opiates in their abilities to produce analgesia and a feeling of well-being.

The term "endorphin" implies a pharmacological activity (analogous to the activity of the corticosteroid category of biochemicals) as opposed to a specific chemical formulation.

Clam101

Chapter 6. ALL AROUNDERS

Epinephrine	Epinephrine is a hormone and a neurotransmitter. It increases heart rate, constricts blood vessels, dilates air passages and participates in the fight-or-flight response of the sympathetic nervous system. Chemically, epinephrine is a catecholamine, a monoamine produced only by the adrenal glands from the amino acids phenylalanine and tyrosine.
Norepinephrine	Norepinephrine is a catecholamine with multiple roles including as a hormone and a neurotransmitter. As a stress hormone, norepinephrine affects parts of the brain, such as the amygdala, where attention and responses are controlled. Along with epinephrine, norepinephrine also underlies the fight-or-flight response, directly increasing heart rate, triggering the release of glucose from energy stores, and increasing blood flow to skeletal muscle. It increases the brain's oxygen supply. Norepinephrine can also suppress neuroinflammation when released diffusely in the brain from the locus ceruleus.
Stimulant	Stimulants are psychoactive drugs which induce temporary improvements in either mental or physical function or both. Examples of these kinds of effects may include enhanced alertness, wakefulness, and locomotion, among others. Due to their effects typically having an "up" quality to them, stimulants are also occasionally referred to as "uppers".
Desipramine	Desipramine is a tricyclic antidepressant (TCA). It inhibits the reuptake of norepinephrine and to a lesser extent serotonin. It is used to treat depression, but not considered a first line treatment since the introduction of SSRI antidepressants. Desipramine is an active metabolite of imipramine.
Substance Abuse	Substance abuse refers to a maladaptive pattern of use of a substance that is not considered dependent. The term "drug abuse" does not exclude dependency, but is otherwise used in a similar manner in nonmedical contexts. The terms have a huge range of definitions related to taking a psychoactive drug or performance enhancing drug for a non-therapeutic or non-medical effect.
Cannabis indica	Cannabis indica is an annual plant in the Cannabaceae family. A putative species of the genus Cannabis, it is typically distinguished from Cannabis sativa.

Chapter 6. ALL AROUNDERS

Hormone	A hormone is a chemical released by a cell or a gland in one part of the body that sends out messages that affect cells in other parts of the organism. Only a small amount of hormone is required to alter cell metabolism. In essence, it is a chemical messenger that transports a signal from one cell to another. All multicellular organisms produce hormones; plant hormones are also called phytohormones. Hormones in animals are often transported in the blood. Cells respond to a hormone when they express a specific receptor for that hormone. The hormone binds to the receptor protein, resulting in the activation of a signal transduction mechanism that ultimately leads to cell type-specific responses.
Amygdala	The amygdalae are almond-shaped groups of nuclei located deep within the medial temporal lobes of the brain in complex vertebrates, including humans. Shown in research to perform a primary role in the processing and memory of emotional reactions, the amygdalae are considered part of the limbic system.
Nucleus accumbens	The nucleus accumbens also known as the accumbens nucleus or as the nucleus accumbens septi, is a collection of neurons within the striatum. It is thought to play an important role in reward, pleasure, laughter, addiction, aggression, fear, and the placebo effect. Each half of the brain has one nucleus accumbens.
Posttraumatic stress disorder	Posttraumatic stress disorder is a severe anxiety disorder that can develop after exposure to any event that results in psychological trauma. This event may involve the threat of death to oneself or to someone else, or to one's own or someone else's physical, sexual, or psychological integrity, overwhelming the individual's ability to cope. As an effect of psychological trauma, Posttraumatic stress disorder is less frequent and more enduring than the more commonly seen acute stress response.
Hypothalamus	The Hypothalamus is a portion of the brain that contains a number of small nuclei with a variety of functions. One of the most important functions of the hypothalamus is to link the nervous system to the endocrine system via the pituitary gland (hypophysis). The hypothalamus is located below the thalamus, just above the brain stem.

Chapter 6. ALL AROUNDERS

Learning	Learning is acquiring new or modifying existing knowledge, behaviors, skills, values, or preferences and may involve synthesizing different types of information. The ability to learn is possessed by humans, animals and some machines. Progress over time tends to follow learning curves.
Depression	Depression, one of the most commonly diagnosed psychiatric disorders, is being diagnosed in increasing numbers in various segments of the population worldwide. Depression in the United States alone affects 17.6 million Americans each year or 1 in 6 people. Depressed patients are at increased risk of type 2 diabetes, cardiovascular disease and suicide. Within the next twenty years depression is expected to become the second leading cause of disability worldwide and the leading cause in high-income nations, including the United States. In approximately 75% of completed suicides the individuals had seen a physician within the prior year before their death, 45%-66% within the prior month. Approximately 33% - 41% of those who completed suicide had contact with mental health services in the prior year, 20% within the prior month.
Major depressive disorder	Major depressive disorder is a mental disorder characterized by an all-encompassing low mood accompanied by low self-esteem, and by loss of interest or pleasure in normally enjoyable activities. This cluster of symptoms (syndrome) was named, described and classified as one of the mood disorders in the 1980 edition of the American Psychiatric Association's diagnostic manual. The term "depression" is ambiguous. It is often used to denote this syndrome but may refer to any or all of the mood disorders. Major depressive disorder is a disabling condition which adversely affects a person's family, work or school life, sleeping and eating habits, and general health.
Tranquilizer	A tranquilizer, is a drug that induces tranquillity in an individual. The term "tranquilizer" is imprecise, and is usually qualified, or replaced with more precise terms: • minor tranquilizer usually refers to anxiolytic or antianxiety agent • major tranquilizer usually refers to antipsychotics

Antimanic agents can also be considered tranquilizing agents.

In music

- "Tranquilizer" is a song written by Tom Stephan ' Neil Tennant, from album Superchumbo "WowieZowie" (2005).

- Tranquilizer by Fat Jon The Ample Soul Physician, from album Repaint Tomorow

.

Chapter 7. OTHER DRUGS, OTHER ADDICTIONS

MDMA	MDMA - colloquially known as ecstasy, often abbreviated "E" or "X" - is an entactogenic drug of the phenethylamine and amphetamine class of drugs.
	MDMA can induce euphoria, a sense of intimacy with others, and diminished anxiety and depression. Many, particularly in the fields of psychology and cognitive therapy, have suggested MDMA might have therapeutic benefits and facilitate therapy sessions in certain individuals, a practice which it had formally been used for in the past.
Butyl nitrite	Butyl nitrite is an alkyl nitrite made from n-butanol. Butyl nitrite is used recreationally as poppers.
	Chemistry
	Synonyms include N-butyl nitrite, 1-butyl nitrite and nitrous acid, butyl ester.
Substance Abuse	Substance abuse refers to a maladaptive pattern of use of a substance that is not considered dependent. The term "drug abuse" does not exclude dependency, but is otherwise used in a similar manner in nonmedical contexts. The terms have a huge range of definitions related to taking a psychoactive drug or performance enhancing drug for a non-therapeutic or non-medical effect.
Alcohol	In chemistry, an alcohol is any organic compound in which a hydroxyl functional group (-OH) is bound to a carbon atom, usually connected to other carbon or hydrogen atoms.
	An important class are the simple acyclic alcohols, the general formula for which is $C_nH_{2n+1}OH$. Of those, ethanol (C_2H_5OH) is the type of alcohol found in alcoholic beverages, and in common speech the word alcohol refers specifically to ethanol.
Halothane	Halothane vapor (trademarked as Fluothane) is an inhalational general anaesthetic. Its IUPAC name is 2-bromo-2-chloro-1,1,1-trifluoroethane. It is the only inhalational anaesthetic agent containing a bromine atom; there are several other halogenated anesthesia agents which lack the bromine atom and do contain the fluorine and chlorine atoms present in halothane.

Chapter 7. OTHER DRUGS, OTHER ADDICTIONS

Isobutyl nitrite	Isobutyl nitrite, $C_4H_9NO_2$, is an alkyl nitrite, an ester of isobutanol and nitrous acid. Its chemical structure is $(CH_3)_2CH-CH_2-O-NO$. Isobutyl nitrite is a pungent colorless liquid. It acts as a vasodilator, and is used as an inhalant recreational drug.
Ketamine	Ketamine is a drug used in human and veterinary medicine. Its hydrochloride salt is sold as Ketanest, Ketaset, and Ketalar. Pharmacologically, ketamine is classified as an NMDA receptor antagonist.
Salvia Divinorum	Salvia divinorum is a psychoactive plant which can induce dissociative effects and is a potent producer of "visions" and other hallucinatory experiences. Its native habitat is within cloud forest in the isolated Sierra Mazateca of Oaxaca, Mexico, growing in shady and moist locations. The plant grows to over a meter high, has hollow square stems, large leaves, and occasional white flowers with violet calyx.
Hallucination	A hallucination, in the broadest sense of the word, is a perception in the absence of a stimulus. In a stricter sense, hallucinations are defined as perceptions in a conscious and awake state in the absence of external stimuli which have qualities of real perception, in that they are vivid, substantial, and located in external objective space. The latter definition distinguishes hallucinations from the related phenomena of dreaming, which does not involve wakefulness; illusion, which involves distorted or misinterpreted real perception; imagery, which does not mimic real perception and is under voluntary control; and pseudohallucination, which does not mimic real perception, but is not under voluntary control.
Brainstem	In vertebrate anatomy the brainstem is the posterior part of the brain, adjoining and structurally continuous with the spinal cord. The brain stem provides the main motor and sensory innervation to the face and neck via the cranial nerves. Though small, this is an extremely important part of the brain as the nerve connections of the motor and sensory systems from the main part of the brain to the rest of the body pass through the brain stem.
Ibogaine	Ibogaine is a naturally occurring psychoactive substance found in a number of plants, principally in a member of the Apocynaceae family known as iboga (Tabernanthe iboga).

131

A hallucinogen, the substance is banned in some countries; in other countries it is being used to treat addiction to opiates, methamphetamine and other drugs. Derivatives of ibogaine that lack the substance's hallucinogen properties are under development.

Kava	Kava is a crop of the western Pacific. The roots of the plant are used to produce a drink with mild sedative properties. Kava is consumed throughout the Pacific Ocean cultures of Polynesia (including Hawaii), Vanuatu, Melanesia and some parts of Micronesia. Kava is sedating and is primarily consumed to relax without disrupting mental clarity. Its active ingredients are called kavalactones.
Khat	Khat is a flowering plant native to tropical East Africa and the Arabian Peninsula. Khat contains the alkaloid called cathinone, an amphetamine-like stimulant which is said to cause excitement, loss of appetite, and euphoria. In 1980, the World Health Organization classified khat as a drug of abuse that can produce mild to moderate psychological dependence (less than tobacco or alcohol). The plant has been targeted by anti-drug organizations like the DEA. It is a controlled or illegal substance in many countries, but is legal for sale and production in many others.
Neurotransmitter	Neurotransmitters are endogenous chemicals which transmit signals from a neuron to a target cell across a synapse. Neurotransmitters are packaged into synaptic vesicles clustered beneath the membrane on the presynaptic side of a synapse, and are released into the synaptic cleft, where they bind to receptors in the membrane on the postsynaptic side of the synapse. Release of neurotransmitters usually follows arrival of an action potential at the synapse, but may also follow graded electrical potentials.
Opium	Opium is the dried latex obtained from the opium poppy (Papaver somniferum). Opium contains up to 12% morphine, an alkaloid, which is frequently processed chemically to produce heroin for the illegal drug trade. The latex also includes codeine and non-narcotic alkaloids such as papaverine, thebaine and noscapine.

Chapter 7. OTHER DRUGS, OTHER ADDICTIONS

Muscle relaxant	A muscle relaxant is a drug which affects skeletal muscle function and decreases the muscle tone. It may be used to alleviate symptoms such as muscle spasms, pain, and hyperreflexia. The term "muscle relaxant" is used to refer to two major therapeutic groups: neuromuscular blockers and spasmolytics. Neuromuscular blockers act by interfering with transmission at the neuromuscular end plate and have no CNS activity. They are often used during surgical procedures and in intensive care and emergency medicine to cause paralysis. Spasmolytics, also known as "centrally-acting" muscle relaxants, are used to alleviate musculoskeletal pain and spasms and to reduce spasticity in a variety of neurological conditions. While both neuromuscular blockers and spasmolytics are often grouped together as muscle relaxants, the term is commonly used to refer to spasmolytics only.
Cocaine	Cocaine benzoylmethylecgonine (INN) is a crystalline tropane alkaloid that is obtained from the leaves of the coca plant. The name comes from "coca" in addition to the alkaloid suffix -ine, forming cocaine. It is a stimulant of the central nervous system, an appetite suppressant, and a topical anesthetic. Specifically, it is a serotonin-norepinephrine-dopamine reuptake inhibitor, which mediates functionality of these neurotransmitters as an exogenous catecholamine transporter ligand. Because of the way it affects the mesolimbic reward pathway, cocaine is addictive.
Ephedrine	Ephedrine is a sympathomimetic amine commonly used as a stimulant, appetite suppressant, concentration aid, decongestant, and to treat hypotension associated with anaesthesia.
	Ephedrine is similar in structure to the (semi-synthetic) derivatives amphetamine and methamphetamine. Chemically, it is an alkaloid derived from various plants in the genus Ephedra (family Ephedraceae). It works mainly by increasing the activity of noradrenaline on adrenergic receptors. It is most usually marketed in the hydrochloride and sulfate forms.
Morpheus	Morpheus in Greek mythology is the god of dreams, leader of the Oneiroi. Morpheus has the ability to take any human form and appear in dreams. His true semblance is that of a winged daemon, imagery shared with many of his siblings.
Anti-inflammatory	Anti-inflammatory refers to the property of a substance or treatment that reduces inflammation. Anti-inflammatory drugs make up about half of analgesics, remedying pain by reducing inflammation as opposed to opioids which affect the central nervous system.

Clonazepam	Clonazepam is a benzodiazepine derivative with anticonvulsant, muscle relaxant, and very potent anxiolytic properties. It is marketed by Roche under the trade-names Klonopin in the United States, and Ravotril in Chile. Other names like Rivotril or Rivatril are known throughout the large majority of the rest of the world. Clonazepam has an unusually long half-life of 18-50 hours, making it generally considered to be among the long-acting benzodiazepines. Clonazepam is a chlorinated derivative of nitrazepam and therefore a nitrobenzodiazepine.
Codeine	Codeine (a natural isomer of methylated morphine, the other being the semi-synthetic 6-methylmorphine) is an opiate used for its analgesic, antitussive, and antidiarrheal properties. Codeine is the second-most predominant alkaloid in opium, at up to 3 percent; it is much more prevalent in the Iranian poppy (Papaver bractreatum), and codeine is extracted from this species in some places although the below-mentioned morphine methylation process is still much more common. It is considered the prototype of the weak to midrange opioids.
Pethidine	Pethidine is a fast-acting opioid analgesic drug. In the United States and Canada, it is more commonly known as meperidine or by its brand name Demerol. Pethidine was the first synthetic opioid synthesized in 1932 as a potential anti-spasmodic agent by the chemist Otto Eislib. Its analgesic properties were first recognized by Otto Schaumann working for IG Farben, Germany.
Morphine	Supplementary data for morphine. Structure and properties
Sulindac	Sulindac is a non-steroidal anti-inflammatory drug of the arylalkanoic acid class that is marketed in the UK ' U.S. by Merck as Clinoril. Like other NSAIDs, it is useful in the treatment of acute or chronic inflammatory conditions. Sulindac is a prodrug, derived from sulfinylindene, that is converted in the body to the active NSAID. More specifically, the agent is converted by liver enzymes to a sulfide that is excreted in the bile and then reabsorbed from the intestine. This is thought to help maintain constant blood levels with reduced gastrointestinal side effects. Some studies have shown sulindac to be relatively less irritating to the stomach than other NSAIDs except for drugs of the COX-2 inhibitor class. The exact mechanism of its NSAID properties is unknown, but it is thought to act on enzymes COX-1 and COX-2, inhibiting prostaglandin synthesis.

Chapter 7. OTHER DRUGS, OTHER ADDICTIONS

Opioid	An opioid is a chemical that works by binding to opioid receptors, which are found principally in the central and peripheral nervous system and the gastrointestinal tract. The receptors in these organ systems mediate both the beneficial effects and the side effects of opioids. Opioids are among the world's oldest known drugs; the use of the opium poppy for its therapeutic benefits predates recorded history.
Stimulant	Stimulants are psychoactive drugs which induce temporary improvements in either mental or physical function or both. Examples of these kinds of effects may include enhanced alertness, wakefulness, and locomotion, among others. Due to their effects typically having an "up" quality to them, stimulants are also occasionally referred to as "uppers".
Cannabis	Cannabis is a genus of flowering plants that includes three putative species, Cannabis sativa, Cannabis indica, and Cannabis ruderalis. These three taxa are indigenous to Central Asia, and South Asia. Cannabis has long been used for fibre (hemp), for seed and seed oils, for medicinal purposes, and as a recreational drug.
Decongestant	A decongestant is a type of drug that is used to relieve nasal congestion. The vast majority of decongestants act via enhancing norepinephrine (noradrenaline) and epinephrine (adrenaline) or adrenergic activity by stimulating the α-adrenergic receptors. This induces vasoconstriction of the blood vessels in the nose, throat, and paranasal sinuses, which results in reduced inflammation (swelling) and mucus formation in these areas.
Phenylpropanolamine	Phenylpropanolamine is a psychoactive drug of the phenethylamine and amphetamine chemical classes which is used as a stimulant, decongestant, and anorectic agent. It is commonly used in prescription and over-the-counter cough and cold preparations. In veterinary medicine, it is used to control urinary incontinence in dogs under trade names Propalin and Proin.

Chapter 7. OTHER DRUGS, OTHER ADDICTIONS

Beta blocker	Beta blockers are a class of drugs used for various indications, but particularly for the management of cardiac arrhythmias, cardioprotection after myocardial infarction (heart attack), and hypertension. As beta adrenergic receptor antagonists, they diminish the effects of epinephrine (adrenaline) and other stress hormones. In 1958 the first beta blocker, dichloroisoproterenol, was synthesised by Eli Lilly Laboratories, but it was Sir James W. Black in 1962, who found the first clinically significant use of beta blockers with propranolol and pronethalol; it revolutionized the medical management of angina pectoris and is considered by many to be one of the most important contributions to clinical medicine and pharmacology of the 20th century.
Estrogen	Estrogens (AmE), oestrogens (BE), or œstrogens, are a group of compounds named for their importance in the estrous cycle of humans and other animals, and functioning as the primary female sex hormones. Natural estrogens are steroid hormones, while some synthetic ones are non-steroidal.
Modafinil	Modafinil is an analeptic drug manufactured by Cephalon, and is approved by the U.S. Food and Drug Administration (FDA) for the treatment of narcolepsy, shift work sleep disorder, and excessive daytime sleepiness associated with obstructive sleep apnea. The European Medicines Agency has recommended that in Europe it be prescribed only for narcolepsy.
Gonadotropin	Gonadotropins (or glycoprotein hormones) are protein hormones secreted by gonadotrope cells of the pituitary gland of vertebrates. This is a family of proteins, which include the mammalian hormones follitropin (FSH), lutropin (LH), thyrotropin (TSH) placental chorionic gonadotropins hCG and eCG and chorionic gonadotropin as well as at least two forms of fish gonadotropins. These hormones are central to the complex endocrine system that regulates normal growth, sexual development, and reproductive function.
Narcolepsy	Narcolepsy is a chronic sleep disorder, or dyssomnia, characterized by excessive daytime sleepiness (EDS) in which a person experiences extreme fatigue and possibly falls asleep at inappropriate times, such as while at work or at school. Narcoleptics usually experience disturbed nocturnal sleep and an abnormal daytime sleep pattern, which is often confused with insomnia. When a narcoleptic falls asleep they generally experience the REM stage of sleep within 10 minutes; whereas most people do not experience REM sleep until after 90 minutes.
Serotonin	Serotonin is a monoamine neurotransmitter. Biochemically derived from tryptophan, serotonin is primarily found in the gastrointestinal (GI) tract, platelets, and in the central nervous system (CNS) of animals including humans. It is a well-known contributor to feelings of well-being; therefore it is also known as a "happiness hormone" despite not being a hormone.

Chapter 7. OTHER DRUGS, OTHER ADDICTIONS

Depressant	Depressants are psychoactive drugs that temporarily reduce the function or activity of a specific part of the body or brain. Examples of these kinds of effects may include anxiolysis, sedation, and hypotension. Due to their effects typically having a "down" quality to them, depressants are also occasionally referred to as "downers".
Acetylcholine	The chemical compound acetylcholine is a neurotransmitter in both the peripheral nervous system (PNS) and central nervous system (CNS) in many organisms including humans. Acetylcholine is one of many neurotransmitters in the autonomic nervous system (ANS) and the only neurotransmitter used in the motor division of the somatic nervous system. (Sensory neurons use glutamate and various peptides at their synapses). Acetylcholine is also the principal neurotransmitter in all autonomic ganglia.
Dopamine	Dopamine is a catecholamine neurotransmitter present in a wide variety of animals, including both vertebrates and invertebrates. In the brain, this substituted phenethylamine functions as a neurotransmitter, activating the five known types of dopamine receptors--D_1, D_2, D_3, D_4, and D_5-- and their variants. Dopamine is produced in several areas of the brain, including the substantia nigra and the ventral tegmental area.
Endorphin	Endorphins ("endogenous morphine") are endogenous opioid peptides that function as neurotransmitters. They are produced by the pituitary gland and the hypothalamus in vertebrates during exercise, excitement, pain, consumption of spicy food, love and orgasm, and they resemble the opiates in their abilities to produce analgesia and a feeling of well-being. The term "endorphin" implies a pharmacological activity (analogous to the activity of the corticosteroid category of biochemicals) as opposed to a specific chemical formulation.
Epinephrine	Epinephrine is a hormone and a neurotransmitter. It increases heart rate, constricts blood vessels, dilates air passages and participates in the fight-or-flight response of the sympathetic nervous system. Chemically, epinephrine is a catecholamine, a monoamine produced only by the adrenal glands from the amino acids phenylalanine and tyrosine.
Ginseng	Ginseng is any one of eleven distinct species of slow-growing perennial plants with fleshy roots, belonging to the Panax genus in the family Araliaceae. It grows in the Northern Hemisphere in eastern Asia (mostly northern China, Korea, and eastern Siberia), typically in cooler climates; Panax vietnamensis, discovered in Vietnam, is the southernmost ginseng found quinquefolius. Ginseng is characterized by the presence of ginsenosides.

Chapter 7. OTHER DRUGS, OTHER ADDICTIONS

Norepinephrine	Norepinephrine is a catecholamine with multiple roles including as a hormone and a neurotransmitter. As a stress hormone, norepinephrine affects parts of the brain, such as the amygdala, where attention and responses are controlled. Along with epinephrine, norepinephrine also underlies the fight-or-flight response, directly increasing heart rate, triggering the release of glucose from energy stores, and increasing blood flow to skeletal muscle. It increases the brain's oxygen supply. Norepinephrine can also suppress neuroinflammation when released diffusely in the brain from the locus ceruleus.
Amygdala	The amygdalae are almond-shaped groups of nuclei located deep within the medial temporal lobes of the brain in complex vertebrates, including humans. Shown in research to perform a primary role in the processing and memory of emotional reactions, the amygdalae are considered part of the limbic system.
Nucleus accumbens	The nucleus accumbens also known as the accumbens nucleus or as the nucleus accumbens septi, is a collection of neurons within the striatum. It is thought to play an important role in reward, pleasure, laughter, addiction, aggression, fear, and the placebo effect. Each half of the brain has one nucleus accumbens.
Alcohol Abuse	Pie abuse, as described in the DSM-IV, is a psychiatric diagnosis describing the recurring use of alcoholic beverages despite negative consequences. Alcohol abuse is sometimes referred to by the less specific term alcoholism. However, many definitions of alcoholism exist, and only some are compatible with alcohol abuse.
Desipramine	Desipramine is a tricyclic antidepressant (TCA). It inhibits the reuptake of norepinephrine and to a lesser extent serotonin. It is used to treat depression, but not considered a first line treatment since the introduction of SSRI antidepressants. Desipramine is an active metabolite of imipramine.
Hypothalamus	The Hypothalamus is a portion of the brain that contains a number of small nuclei with a variety of functions. One of the most important functions of the hypothalamus is to link the nervous system to the endocrine system via the pituitary gland (hypophysis).

The hypothalamus is located below the thalamus, just above the brain stem.

Insulin	Insulin is a hormone that is central to regulating carbohydrate and fat metabolism in the body. Insulin causes cells in the liver, muscle, and fat tissue to take up glucose from the blood, storing it as glycogen in the liver and muscle. Insulin stops the use of fat as an energy source by inhibiting the release of glucagon. When insulin is absent, glucose is not taken up by body cells and the body begins to use fat as an energy source or gluconeogenesis; for example, by transfer of lipids from adipose tissue to the liver for mobilization as an energy source. As its level is a central metabolic control mechanism, its status is also used as a control signal to other body systems (such as amino acid uptake by body cells). In addition, it has several other anabolic effects throughout the body.
Amenorrhoea	Amenorrhoea is the absence of a menstrual period in a woman of reproductive age. Physiological states of amenorrhoea are seen during pregnancy and lactation (breastfeeding), the latter also forming the basis of a form of contraception known as the lactational amenorrhoea method. Outside of the reproductive years there is absence of menses during childhood and after menopause.
Dopaminergic	Dopaminergic means related to the neurotransmitter dopamine. For example, certain proteins such as the dopamine transporter (DAT), vesicular monoamine transporter 2 ($VMAT_2$), and dopamine receptors can be classified as dopaminergic, and neurons which synthesize or contain dopamine and synapses with dopamine receptors in them may also be labeled as dopaminergic. Enzymes which regulate the biosynthesis or metabolism of dopamine such as aromatic L-amino acid decarboxylase (AAAD) or DOPA decarboxylase (DDC), monoamine oxidase (MAO), and catechol O-methyl transferase (COMT) may be referred to as dopaminergic as well.
Fluoxetine	Fluoxetine is an antidepressant of the selective serotonin reuptake inhibitor (SSRI) class. It is manufactured and marketed by Eli Lilly and Company. In combination with olanzapine it is known as symbyax. Fluoxetine is approved for the treatment of major depression (including pediatric depression), obsessive-compulsive disorder (in both adult and pediatric populations), bulimia nervosa, panic disorder and premenstrual dysphoric disorder.

Chapter 8. DRUG USE & PREVENTION: FROM CRADLE TO GRAVE

Salvia divinorum	Salvia divinorum is a psychoactive plant which can induce dissociative effects and is a potent producer of "visions" and other hallucinatory experiences. Its native habitat is within cloud forest in the isolated Sierra Mazateca of Oaxaca, Mexico, growing in shady and moist locations. The plant grows to over a meter high, has hollow square stems, large leaves, and occasional white flowers with violet calyx.
Serotonin	Serotonin is a monoamine neurotransmitter. Biochemically derived from tryptophan, serotonin is primarily found in the gastrointestinal (GI) tract, platelets, and in the central nervous system (CNS) of animals including humans. It is a well-known contributor to feelings of well-being; therefore it is also known as a "happiness hormone" despite not being a hormone.
Alcohol	In chemistry, an alcohol is any organic compound in which a hydroxyl functional group (-OH) is bound to a carbon atom, usually connected to other carbon or hydrogen atoms. An important class are the simple acyclic alcohols, the general formula for which is $C_nH_{2n+1}OH$. Of those, ethanol (C_2H_5OH) is the type of alcohol found in alcoholic beverages, and in common speech the word alcohol refers specifically to ethanol.
Opium	Opium is the dried latex obtained from the opium poppy (Papaver somniferum). Opium contains up to 12% morphine, an alkaloid, which is frequently processed chemically to produce heroin for the illegal drug trade. The latex also includes codeine and non-narcotic alkaloids such as papaverine, thebaine and noscapine.
COCAINE	Cocaine benzoylmethylecgonine (INN) is a crystalline tropane alkaloid that is obtained from the leaves of the coca plant. The name comes from "coca" in addition to the alkaloid suffix -ine, forming cocaine. It is a stimulant of the central nervous system, an appetite suppressant, and a topical anesthetic. Specifically, it is a serotonin-norepinephrine-dopamine reuptake inhibitor, which mediates functionality of these neurotransmitters as an exogenous catecholamine transporter ligand. Because of the way it affects the mesolimbic reward pathway, cocaine is addictive.
MDMA	MDMA - colloquially known as ecstasy, often abbreviated "E" or "X" - is an entactogenic drug of the phenethylamine and amphetamine class of drugs.

149

MDMA can induce euphoria, a sense of intimacy with others, and diminished anxiety and depression. Many, particularly in the fields of psychology and cognitive therapy, have suggested MDMA might have therapeutic benefits and facilitate therapy sessions in certain individuals, a practice which it had formally been used for in the past.

Desipramine	Desipramine is a tricyclic antidepressant (TCA). It inhibits the reuptake of norepinephrine and to a lesser extent serotonin. It is used to treat depression, but not considered a first line treatment since the introduction of SSRI antidepressants. Desipramine is an active metabolite of imipramine.
Posttraumatic stress disorder	Posttraumatic stress disorder is a severe anxiety disorder that can develop after exposure to any event that results in psychological trauma. This event may involve the threat of death to oneself or to someone else, or to one's own or someone else's physical, sexual, or psychological integrity, overwhelming the individual's ability to cope. As an effect of psychological trauma, Posttraumatic stress disorder is less frequent and more enduring than the more commonly seen acute stress response.
Narcotic	The term narcotic originally referred medically to any psychoactive compound with sleep-inducing properties. In the United States of America it has since become associated with opioids, commonly morphine and heroin. The term is, today, imprecisely defined and typically has negative connotations.
Designer drug	Designer drug is a term used to describe drugs which are created (or marketed, if they had already existed) to get around existing drug laws, usually by modifying the molecular structures of existing drugs to varying degrees, or less commonly by finding drugs with entirely different chemical structures that produce similar subjective effects to illegal recreational drugs.

History

United States

1920s-1930s |

Chapter 8. DRUG USE & PREVENTION: FROM CRADLE TO GRAVE

	The term "designer drug" was first coined by law enforcement in the 1980s, and has gained widespread use. However the first appearance of what would now be termed designer drugs occurred well before this, in the 1920s.
Ephedrine	Ephedrine is a sympathomimetic amine commonly used as a stimulant, appetite suppressant, concentration aid, decongestant, and to treat hypotension associated with anaesthesia.
	Ephedrine is similar in structure to the (semi-synthetic) derivatives amphetamine and methamphetamine. Chemically, it is an alkaloid derived from various plants in the genus Ephedra (family Ephedraceae). It works mainly by increasing the activity of noradrenaline on adrenergic receptors. It is most usually marketed in the hydrochloride and sulfate forms.
Substance abuse	Substance abuse refers to a maladaptive pattern of use of a substance that is not considered dependent. The term "drug abuse" does not exclude dependency, but is otherwise used in a similar manner in nonmedical contexts. The terms have a huge range of definitions related to taking a psychoactive drug or performance enhancing drug for a non-therapeutic or non-medical effect.
Alcohol Abuse	Pie abuse, as described in the DSM-IV, is a psychiatric diagnosis describing the recurring use of alcoholic beverages despite negative consequences. Alcohol abuse is sometimes referred to by the less specific term alcoholism. However, many definitions of alcoholism exist, and only some are compatible with alcohol abuse.
Morpheus	Morpheus in Greek mythology is the god of dreams, leader of the Oneiroi. Morpheus has the ability to take any human form and appear in dreams. His true semblance is that of a winged daemon, imagery shared with many of his siblings.
Morphine	Supplementary data for morphine. Structure and properties
Opioid	An opioid is a chemical that works by binding to opioid receptors, which are found principally in the central and peripheral nervous system and the gastrointestinal tract. The receptors in these organ systems mediate both the beneficial effects and the side effects of opioids.

Chapter 8. DRUG USE & PREVENTION: FROM CRADLE TO GRAVE

	Opioids are among the world's oldest known drugs; the use of the opium poppy for its therapeutic benefits predates recorded history.
Stimulant	Stimulants are psychoactive drugs which induce temporary improvements in either mental or physical function or both. Examples of these kinds of effects may include enhanced alertness, wakefulness, and locomotion, among others. Due to their effects typically having an "up" quality to them, stimulants are also occasionally referred to as "uppers".
Methamphetamine	Methamphetamine, methylamphetamine, N-methylamphetamine, desoxyephedrine, and colloquially as "meth" or "crystal meth", is a psychostimulant of the phenethylamine and amphetamine class of drugs. It increases alertness, concentration, energy, and in high doses, can induce euphoria, enhance self-esteem, and increase libido. Methamphetamine has high potential for abuse and addiction by activating the psychological reward system via triggering a cascading release of dopamine, norepinephrine and serotonin in the brain.
Estrogen	Estrogens (AmE), oestrogens (BE), or œstrogens, are a group of compounds named for their importance in the estrous cycle of humans and other animals, and functioning as the primary female sex hormones. Natural estrogens are steroid hormones, while some synthetic ones are non-steroidal.
Limbic system	The limbic system is a set of brain structures including the hippocampus, amygdala, anterior thalamic nuclei, septum, limbic cortex and fornix, which seemingly support a variety of functions including emotion, behavior, long term memory, and olfaction. The term "limbic" comes from the Latin limbus, for "border" or "edge". Some scientists have suggested that the concept of the limbic system should be abandoned as obsolete, as it is grounded more in transient tradition than in facts.
Cannabis	Cannabis is a genus of flowering plants that includes three putative species, Cannabis sativa, Cannabis indica, and Cannabis ruderalis. These three taxa are indigenous to Central Asia, and South Asia. Cannabis has long been used for fibre (hemp), for seed and seed oils, for medicinal purposes, and as a recreational drug.
Dopamine	Dopamine is a catecholamine neurotransmitter present in a wide variety of animals, including both vertebrates and invertebrates. In the brain, this substituted phenethylamine functions as a neurotransmitter, activating the five known types of dopamine receptors--D_1, D_2, D_3, D_4, and D_5-- and their variants. Dopamine is produced in several areas of the brain, including the substantia nigra and the ventral tegmental area.

Chapter 8. DRUG USE & PREVENTION: FROM CRADLE TO GRAVE

Antipsychotic	An antipsychotic is a tranquilizing psychiatric medication primarily used to manage psychosis (including delusions or hallucinations, as well as disordered thought), particularly in schizophrenia and bipolar disorder. A first generation of antipsychotics, known as typical antipsychotics, was discovered in the 1950s. Most of the drugs in the second generation, known as atypical antipsychotics, have been developed more recently, although the first atypical antipsychotic, clozapine, was discovered in the 1950s and introduced clinically in the 1970s.
Fluoxetine	Fluoxetine is an antidepressant of the selective serotonin reuptake inhibitor (SSRI) class. It is manufactured and marketed by Eli Lilly and Company. In combination with olanzapine it is known as symbyax. Fluoxetine is approved for the treatment of major depression (including pediatric depression), obsessive-compulsive disorder (in both adult and pediatric populations), bulimia nervosa, panic disorder and premenstrual dysphoric disorder.
Isobutyl nitrite	Isobutyl nitrite, $C_4H_9NO_2$, is an alkyl nitrite, an ester of isobutanol and nitrous acid. Its chemical structure is $(CH_3)_2CH\text{-}CH_2\text{-}O\text{-}NO$. Isobutyl nitrite is a pungent colorless liquid. It acts as a vasodilator, and is used as an inhalant recreational drug.
Psychiatric medication	A psychiatric medication is a licensed psychoactive drug taken to exert an effect on the mental state and used to treat mental disorders. Usually prescribed in psychiatric settings, these medications are typically made of synthetic chemical compounds, although some are naturally occurring, or at least naturally derived. Administration Prescription psychiatric medications, like all prescription medications, require a prescription from a physician, such as a psychiatrist, or a psychiatric nurse practitioner, PMHNP, before they can be obtained.

Chapter 8. DRUG USE & PREVENTION: FROM CRADLE TO GRAVE

Neurotransmitter	Neurotransmitters are endogenous chemicals which transmit signals from a neuron to a target cell across a synapse. Neurotransmitters are packaged into synaptic vesicles clustered beneath the membrane on the presynaptic side of a synapse, and are released into the synaptic cleft, where they bind to receptors in the membrane on the postsynaptic side of the synapse. Release of neurotransmitters usually follows arrival of an action potential at the synapse, but may also follow graded electrical potentials.
Hallucinogen persisting perception disorder	Hallucinogen persisting perception disorder are reminiscent of those generated by the ingestion of hallucinogenic substances. Previous use of hallucinogens by the person is needed, though not sufficient, for diagnosing someone with the disorder. For an individual to be diagnosed with Hallucinogen persisting perception disorder, the symptoms cannot be due to another medical condition.
Perception	In philosophy, psychology, and cognitive science, perception is the process of attaining awareness or understanding of sensory information. The word "perception" comes from the Latin words perceptio, percipio, and means "receiving, collecting, action of taking possession, apprehension with the mind or senses."
	Perception is one of the oldest fields in psychology. The oldest quantitative law in psychology is the Weber-Fechner law, which quantifies the relationship between the intensity of physical stimuli and their perceptual effects.
Clonazepam	Clonazepam is a benzodiazepine derivative with anticonvulsant, muscle relaxant, and very potent anxiolytic properties. It is marketed by Roche under the trade-names Klonopin in the United States, and Ravotril in Chile. Other names like Rivotril or Rivatril are known throughout the large majority of the rest of the world. Clonazepam has an unusually long half-life of 18-50 hours, making it generally considered to be among the long-acting benzodiazepines. Clonazepam is a chlorinated derivative of nitrazepam and therefore a nitrobenzodiazepine.
Codeine	Codeine (a natural isomer of methylated morphine, the other being the semi-synthetic 6-methylmorphine) is an opiate used for its analgesic, antitussive, and antidiarrheal properties. Codeine is the second-most predominant alkaloid in opium, at up to 3 percent; it is much more prevalent in the Iranian poppy (Papaver bractreatum), and codeine is extracted from this species in some places although the below-mentioned morphine methylation process is still much more common. It is considered the prototype of the weak to midrange opioids.

Chapter 8. DRUG USE & PREVENTION: FROM CRADLE TO GRAVE

Pentobarbital	Pentobarbital is a short-acting barbiturate that was first synthesized in 1928. Pentobarbital is available as both a free acid and a sodium salt, the former of which is only slightly soluble in water and ethanol. One trade name for this drug is Nembutal, coined by Dr. John S. Lundy, who started using it in 1930, from the structural formula of the sodium salt--Na (sodium) + ethyl + methyl + butyl + al (common suffix for barbiturates).
Psychopharmacology	Psychopharmacology is the study of drug-induced changes in mood, sensation, thinking, and behavior.
	The field of psychopharmacology studies a wide range of substances with various types of psychoactive properties. The professional and commercial fields of pharmacology and psychopharmacology do not mainly focus on psychedelic or recreational drugs, as the majority of studies are conducted for the development, study, and use of drugs for the modification of behavior and the alleviation of symptoms, particularly in the treatment of mental disorders (psychiatric medication).
Triazolam	Triazolam is a benzodiazepine derivative drug. It possesses pharmacological properties similar to that of other benzodiazepines, but it is generally only used as a sedative to treat severe insomnia. In addition to the hypnotic properties triazolam possesses, amnesic, anxiolytic, sedative, anticonvulsant and muscle relaxant properties are also present. Due to its short half-life, triazolam is not effective for patients that suffer from frequent awakenings or early wakening.
Histamine antagonist	A histamine antagonist is an agent that inhibits action of histamine via histamine receptors. H_1 antihistamines are used as treatment for symptoms of allergies, such as runny nose. Allergies are caused by an excessive type 1 hypersensitivity response of the body to allergens, such as pollen released by plants. An allergic reaction, which if severe enough can lead to anaphylaxis, results in excessive release of histamines and other mediators by the body. Other uses of H_1 antihistamines help with symptoms of local inflammation that result from various conditions, such as insect stings, even if there is no allergic reaction. Other commonly used examples of antihistamines include the H_2 antagonists (cimetidine), which are widely used for the treatment of acid reflux and stomach ulcers, as they decrease gastric acid production.

Chapter 9. TREATMENT

Anxiety disorder	Anxiety disorders are blanket terms covering several different forms of abnormal and pathological fear and anxiety which only came under the aegis of psychiatry at the very end of the 19th century. Gelder, Mayou ' Geddes (2005) explains that anxiety disorders are classified in two groups: continuous symptoms and episodic symptoms. Current psychiatric diagnostic criteria recognize a wide variety of anxiety disorders.
MDMA	MDMA - colloquially known as ecstasy, often abbreviated "E" or "X" - is an entactogenic drug of the phenethylamine and amphetamine class of drugs.
	MDMA can induce euphoria, a sense of intimacy with others, and diminished anxiety and depression. Many, particularly in the fields of psychology and cognitive therapy, have suggested MDMA might have therapeutic benefits and facilitate therapy sessions in certain individuals, a practice which it had formally been used for in the past.
Alcohol	In chemistry, an alcohol is any organic compound in which a hydroxyl functional group (-OH) is bound to a carbon atom, usually connected to other carbon or hydrogen atoms.
	An important class are the simple acyclic alcohols, the general formula for which is $C_nH_{2n+1}OH$. Of those, ethanol (C_2H_5OH) is the type of alcohol found in alcoholic beverages, and in common speech the word alcohol refers specifically to ethanol.
Bromocriptine	Bromocriptine an ergoline derivative, is a dopamine agonist that is used in the treatment of pituitary tumors, Parkinson's disease (PD), hyperprolactinaemia, neuroleptic malignant syndrome, and type 2 diabetes.
	Indications
	Amenorrhea, female infertility, galactorrhea, hypogonadism, and acromegaly may all be caused by pituitary problems, such as hyperprolactinaemia, and therefore, these problems may be treated by this drug. In 2009, bromocriptine mesylate was approved by the FDA for treatment of type 2 diabetes under the trade name Cycloset (VeroScience).

Desipramine	Desipramine is a tricyclic antidepressant (TCA). It inhibits the reuptake of norepinephrine and to a lesser extent serotonin. It is used to treat depression, but not considered a first line treatment since the introduction of SSRI antidepressants. Desipramine is an active metabolite of imipramine.
Fluoxetine	Fluoxetine is an antidepressant of the selective serotonin reuptake inhibitor (SSRI) class. It is manufactured and marketed by Eli Lilly and Company. In combination with olanzapine it is known as symbyax. Fluoxetine is approved for the treatment of major depression (including pediatric depression), obsessive-compulsive disorder (in both adult and pediatric populations), bulimia nervosa, panic disorder and premenstrual dysphoric disorder.
Magnesium citrate	Magnesium citrate, a magnesium salt of citric acid, is a chemical agent used medicinally as a saline laxative and to empty the bowel prior to a surgery or colonoscopy. It is available without a prescription, both as a generic brand or under the brand name Citromag or Citroma. It is also used as a magnesium supplement in pills. The magnesium content of magnesium citrate corresponds to about 11% by mass.
Stimulant	Stimulants are psychoactive drugs which induce temporary improvements in either mental or physical function or both. Examples of these kinds of effects may include enhanced alertness, wakefulness, and locomotion, among others. Due to their effects typically having an "up" quality to them, stimulants are also occasionally referred to as "uppers".
Dopamine	Dopamine is a catecholamine neurotransmitter present in a wide variety of animals, including both vertebrates and invertebrates. In the brain, this substituted phenethylamine functions as a neurotransmitter, activating the five known types of dopamine receptors--D_1, D_2, D_3, D_4, and D_5-- and their variants. Dopamine is produced in several areas of the brain, including the substantia nigra and the ventral tegmental area.
Methylphenidate	Methylphenidate is a psychostimulant drug approved for treatment of attention-deficit hyperactivity disorder, postural orthostatic tachycardia syndrome, and narcolepsy. It may also be prescribed for off-label use in treatment-resistant cases of lethargy, depression, neural insult, obesity, and rarely other psychiatric disorders such as obsessive-compulsive disorder. Methylphenidate belongs to the piperidine class of compounds and increases the levels of dopamine and norepinephrine in the brain through reuptake inhibition of the monoamine transporters. It also increases the release of dopamine and norepinephrine. MPH possesses structural similarities to amphetamine, and, though it is less potent, its pharmacological effects are even more closely related to those of cocaine.

Substance Abuse	Substance abuse refers to a maladaptive pattern of use of a substance that is not considered dependent. The term "drug abuse" does not exclude dependency, but is otherwise used in a similar manner in nonmedical contexts. The terms have a huge range of definitions related to taking a psychoactive drug or performance enhancing drug for a non-therapeutic or non-medical effect.
Twins Early Development Study	The Twins Early Development Study is an ongoing longitudinal twin study, headed by principal investigator and leading psychologist Professor Robert Plomin. The main goal of Twins Early Development Study is to use behavioural genetic methods to find out how nature (genes) and nurture (environments) can explain why people differ with respect to their cognitive abilities, learning abilities and behaviours. Over 15,000 pairs of twins originally signed up for the study and more than 13,000 pairs remain involved to the present day.
Serotonin	Serotonin is a monoamine neurotransmitter. Biochemically derived from tryptophan, serotonin is primarily found in the gastrointestinal (GI) tract, platelets, and in the central nervous system (CNS) of animals including humans. It is a well-known contributor to feelings of well-being; therefore it is also known as a "happiness hormone" despite not being a hormone.
Alcohol Abuse	Pie abuse, as described in the DSM-IV, is a psychiatric diagnosis describing the recurring use of alcoholic beverages despite negative consequences. Alcohol abuse is sometimes referred to by the less specific term alcoholism. However, many definitions of alcoholism exist, and only some are compatible with alcohol abuse.
Narcotic	The term narcotic originally referred medically to any psychoactive compound with sleep-inducing properties. In the United States of America it has since become associated with opioids, commonly morphine and heroin. The term is, today, imprecisely defined and typically has negative connotations.
Opioid	An opioid is a chemical that works by binding to opioid receptors, which are found principally in the central and peripheral nervous system and the gastrointestinal tract. The receptors in these organ systems mediate both the beneficial effects and the side effects of opioids. Opioids are among the world's oldest known drugs; the use of the opium poppy for its therapeutic benefits predates recorded history.

Chapter 9. TREATMENT

Methamphetamine	Methamphetamine, methylamphetamine, N-methylamphetamine, desoxyephedrine, and colloquially as "meth" or "crystal meth", is a psychostimulant of the phenethylamine and amphetamine class of drugs. It increases alertness, concentration, energy, and in high doses, can induce euphoria, enhance self-esteem, and increase libido. Methamphetamine has high potential for abuse and addiction by activating the psychological reward system via triggering a cascading release of dopamine, norepinephrine and serotonin in the brain.
Salvia divinorum	Salvia divinorum is a psychoactive plant which can induce dissociative effects and is a potent producer of "visions" and other hallucinatory experiences. Its native habitat is within cloud forest in the isolated Sierra Mazateca of Oaxaca, Mexico, growing in shady and moist locations. The plant grows to over a meter high, has hollow square stems, large leaves, and occasional white flowers with violet calyx.
Cocaine	Cocaine benzoylmethylecgonine (INN) is a crystalline tropane alkaloid that is obtained from the leaves of the coca plant. The name comes from "coca" in addition to the alkaloid suffix -ine, forming cocaine. It is a stimulant of the central nervous system, an appetite suppressant, and a topical anesthetic. Specifically, it is a serotonin-norepinephrine-dopamine reuptake inhibitor, which mediates functionality of these neurotransmitters as an exogenous catecholamine transporter ligand. Because of the way it affects the mesolimbic reward pathway, cocaine is addictive.
Depression	Depression, one of the most commonly diagnosed psychiatric disorders, is being diagnosed in increasing numbers in various segments of the population worldwide. Depression in the United States alone affects 17.6 million Americans each year or 1 in 6 people. Depressed patients are at increased risk of type 2 diabetes, cardiovascular disease and suicide. Within the next twenty years depression is expected to become the second leading cause of disability worldwide and the leading cause in high-income nations, including the United States. In approximately 75% of completed suicides the individuals had seen a physician within the prior year before their death, 45%-66% within the prior month. Approximately 33% - 41% of those who completed suicide had contact with mental health services in the prior year, 20% within the prior month.
Clonidine	Clonidine is a medication used to treat several medical conditions. It is a direct-acting α_2 adrenergic agonist and an imidazoline. It has been prescribed historically as an antihypertensive drug. It has found new uses, including treatment of some types of neuropathic pain, opioid detoxification, sleep hyperhidrosis, anaesthetic use, and off-label, to counter the side effects of stimulant medications such as methylphenidate or amphetamine. It is becoming a more accepted treatment for insomnia, as well as for relief of menopausal symptoms.

Chapter 9. TREATMENT

Naltrexone	Naltrexone is an opioid receptor antagonist used primarily in the management of alcohol dependence and opioid dependence. It is marketed in generic form as its hydrochloride salt, naltrexone hydrochloride, and marketed under the trade names Revia and Depade. In some countries including the United States, a once-monthly extended-release injectable formulation is marketed under the trade name Vivitrol. Also in the US, Methylnaltrexone Bromide, a closely related drug, is marketed as Relistor, for the treatment of opioid induced constipation.
Amantadine	Amantadine is the organic compound known formally as 1-adamantylamine or 1-aminoadamantane. The molecule consists of adamantane backbone that is substituted at one of the four methyne positions with an amino group. This compound is sold under the name Symmetrel for use both as an antiviral and an antiparkinsonian drug. Rimantadine is a closely related derivative of adamantane with similar biological properties.
Imipramine	Imipramine is an antidepressant medication, a tricyclic antidepressant of the dibenzazepine group. Imipramine is mainly used in the treatment of major depression and enuresis (inability to control urination). It has also been evaluated for use in panic disorder.
Naloxone	Naloxone is a drug used to counter the effects of opiate overdose, for example heroin or morphine overdose. Naloxone is specifically used to counteract life-threatening depression of the central nervous system and respiratory system. Naloxone is also experimentally used in the treatment for congenital insensitivity to pain with anhidrosis (CIPA), an extremely rare disorder (1 in 125 million) that renders one unable to feel pain. It is marketed under various trademarks including Narcan, Nalone, and Narcanti, and has sometimes been mistakenly called "naltrexate." It is not to be confused with naltrexone, an opioid receptor antagonist with qualitatively different effects, used for dependence treatment rather than emergency overdose treatment.
Tryptophan	Tryptophan is one of the 20 standard amino acids, as well as an essential amino acid in the human diet. It is encoded in the standard genetic code as the codon UGG. The slight mispronunciation "tWiptophan" can be used as a mnemonic for its single letter IUPAC code W. Only the L-stereoisomer of tryptophan is used in structural or enzyme proteins, but the D-stereoisomer is occasionally found in naturally produced peptides (for example, the marine venom peptide contryphan). The distinguishing structural characteristic of tryptophan is that it contains an indole functional group. It is an essential amino acid as demonstrated by its growth effects on rats.

Chapter 9. TREATMENT

Norepinephrine	Norepinephrine is a catecholamine with multiple roles including as a hormone and a neurotransmitter. As a stress hormone, norepinephrine affects parts of the brain, such as the amygdala, where attention and responses are controlled. Along with epinephrine, norepinephrine also underlies the fight-or-flight response, directly increasing heart rate, triggering the release of glucose from energy stores, and increasing blood flow to skeletal muscle. It increases the brain's oxygen supply. Norepinephrine can also suppress neuroinflammation when released diffusely in the brain from the locus ceruleus.
Morpheus	Morpheus in Greek mythology is the god of dreams, leader of the Oneiroi. Morpheus has the ability to take any human form and appear in dreams. His true semblance is that of a winged daemon, imagery shared with many of his siblings.
Antipsychotic	An antipsychotic is a tranquilizing psychiatric medication primarily used to manage psychosis (including delusions or hallucinations, as well as disordered thought), particularly in schizophrenia and bipolar disorder. A first generation of antipsychotics, known as typical antipsychotics, was discovered in the 1950s. Most of the drugs in the second generation, known as atypical antipsychotics, have been developed more recently, although the first atypical antipsychotic, clozapine, was discovered in the 1950s and introduced clinically in the 1970s.
Chloral hydrate	Chloral hydrate is a sedative and hypnotic drug as well as a chemical reagent and precursor. The name chloral hydrate indicates that it is formed from chloral (trichloroacetaldehyde) by the addition of one molecule of water. Its chemical formula is $C_2H_3Cl_3O_2$.
Chlordiazepoxide	Chlordiazepoxide, is a sedative/hypnotic drug and benzodiazepine derivative. It is marketed under the trade names Klopoxid, Librax (also contains clidinium bromide), Libritabs, Librium, Mesural, Multum, Novapam, Risolid, Silibrin, Sonimen, Tropium, and Zetran. Chlordiazepoxide was the first benzodiazepine to be synthesised and the discovery of chlordiazepoxide was by pure chance. Chlordiazepoxide and other benzodiazepines were initially accepted with widespread public approval but were followed with widespread public disapproval and recommendations for more restrictive medical guidelines for its use.
Citalopram	Citalopram is an antidepressant drug of the selective serotonin reuptake inhibitor (SSRI) class. It has U.S. Food and Drug Administration (FDA) approval to treat major depression, and is prescribed off-label for a number of anxiety conditions.

Nefazodone	Nefazodone is an antidepressant marketed by Bristol-Myers Squibb. Its sale was discontinued in 2003 in some countries due to the rare incidence of hepatotoxicity (liver damage), which could lead to the need for a liver transplant, or even death. The incidence of severe liver damage is approximately 1 in every 250,000 to 300,000 patient-years. On May 20, 2004, Bristol-Myers Squibb discontinued the sale of Serzone in the United States and Canada. Several generic formulations of nefazodone are still available.
Quetiapine	Quetiapine, marketed by AstraZeneca as Seroquel and by Orion Pharma as Ketipinor, is an atypical antipsychotic approved for the treatment of schizophrenia, acute episodes of bipolar disorder (manic, mixed or depressive), and as an augmentor for the maintenance treatment of depression and bipolar disorder. Annual sales are approximately $4.7 billion worldwide, and $2.9 billion in the U.S. The patent in the U.S., which was set to expire in 2011, received a pediatric exclusivity extension, which pushed its expiration to March 26, 2012. The patent has already expired in Canada. There are now several generic versions of quetiapine, such as Quepin made by Specifar ABEE, Athens, Greece.
Limbic system	The limbic system is a set of brain structures including the hippocampus, amygdala, anterior thalamic nuclei, septum, limbic cortex and fornix, which seemingly support a variety of functions including emotion, behavior, long term memory, and olfaction. The term "limbic" comes from the Latin limbus, for "border" or "edge". Some scientists have suggested that the concept of the limbic system should be abandoned as obsolete, as it is grounded more in transient tradition than in facts.
Modafinil	Modafinil is an analeptic drug manufactured by Cephalon, and is approved by the U.S. Food and Drug Administration (FDA) for the treatment of narcolepsy, shift work sleep disorder, and excessive daytime sleepiness associated with obstructive sleep apnea. The European Medicines Agency has recommended that in Europe it be prescribed only for narcolepsy.
Narcolepsy	Narcolepsy is a chronic sleep disorder, or dyssomnia, characterized by excessive daytime sleepiness (EDS) in which a person experiences extreme fatigue and possibly falls asleep at inappropriate times, such as while at work or at school. Narcoleptics usually experience disturbed nocturnal sleep and an abnormal daytime sleep pattern, which is often confused with insomnia. When a narcoleptic falls asleep they generally experience the REM stage of sleep within 10 minutes; whereas most people do not experience REM sleep until after 90 minutes.

Chapter 9. TREATMENT

Nucleus accumbens	The nucleus accumbens also known as the accumbens nucleus or as the nucleus accumbens septi, is a collection of neurons within the striatum. It is thought to play an important role in reward, pleasure, laughter, addiction, aggression, fear, and the placebo effect. Each half of the brain has one nucleus accumbens.
Cannabis	Cannabis is a genus of flowering plants that includes three putative species, Cannabis sativa, Cannabis indica, and Cannabis ruderalis. These three taxa are indigenous to Central Asia, and South Asia. Cannabis has long been used for fibre (hemp), for seed and seed oils, for medicinal purposes, and as a recreational drug.
Opium	Opium is the dried latex obtained from the opium poppy (Papaver somniferum). Opium contains up to 12% morphine, an alkaloid, which is frequently processed chemically to produce heroin for the illegal drug trade. The latex also includes codeine and non-narcotic alkaloids such as papaverine, thebaine and noscapine.
Muscle relaxant	A muscle relaxant is a drug which affects skeletal muscle function and decreases the muscle tone. It may be used to alleviate symptoms such as muscle spasms, pain, and hyperreflexia. The term "muscle relaxant" is used to refer to two major therapeutic groups: neuromuscular blockers and spasmolytics. Neuromuscular blockers act by interfering with transmission at the neuromuscular end plate and have no CNS activity. They are often used during surgical procedures and in intensive care and emergency medicine to cause paralysis. Spasmolytics, also known as "centrally-acting" muscle relaxants, are used to alleviate musculoskeletal pain and spasms and to reduce spasticity in a variety of neurological conditions. While both neuromuscular blockers and spasmolytics are often grouped together as muscle relaxants, the term is commonly used to refer to spasmolytics only.
Barbiturate	Barbiturates are drugs that act as central nervous system depressants, and, by virtue of this, they produce a wide spectrum of effects, from mild sedation to total anesthesia. They are also effective as anxiolytics, as hypnotics, and as anticonvulsants. They have addiction potential, both physical and psychological. Barbiturates have now largely been replaced by benzodiazepines in routine medical practice - for example, in the treatment of anxiety and insomnia - mainly because benzodiazepines are significantly less dangerous in overdose. However, barbiturates are still used in general anesthesia, as well as for epilepsy. Barbiturates are derivatives of barbituric acid.

Chapter 9. TREATMENT

Butabarbital	Butabarbital is a prescription barbiturate sleep aid. Butabarbital has a particularly fast onset of effects and short duration of action compared to other barbiturates, which makes it useful for certain applications such as treating severe insomnia and relieving anxiety before surgical procedures; however it is also relatively dangerous particularly when combined with alcohol, and so is now rarely used, although it is still prescribed in some Eastern European and South American countries. Its intermediate duration of action gives butabarbital an abuse potential slightly lower than secobarbital.
Carbamazepine	Carbamazepine is an anticonvulsant and mood stabilizing drug used primarily in the treatment of epilepsy and bipolar disorder, as well as trigeminal neuralgia. It is also used off-label for a variety of indications, including attention-deficit hyperactivity disorder (ADHD), schizophrenia, phantom limb syndrome, paroxysmal extreme pain disorder, neuromyotonia, and post-traumatic stress disorder. It has been seen as safe for pregnant women to use carbamazepine as a mood stabilizer.
Gabapentin	Gabapentin is a pharmaceutical drug, specifically a GABA analogue. It was originally developed for the treatment of epilepsy, and currently, gabapentin is widely used to relieve pain, especially neuropathic pain, as well as major depressive disorder. Gabapentin was initially synthesized to mimic the chemical structure of the neurotransmitter gamma-aminobutyric acid (GABA), but is not believed to act on the same brain receptors.
Hallucination	A hallucination, in the broadest sense of the word, is a perception in the absence of a stimulus. In a stricter sense, hallucinations are defined as perceptions in a conscious and awake state in the absence of external stimuli which have qualities of real perception, in that they are vivid, substantial, and located in external objective space. The latter definition distinguishes hallucinations from the related phenomena of dreaming, which does not involve wakefulness; illusion, which involves distorted or misinterpreted real perception; imagery, which does not mimic real perception and is under voluntary control; and pseudohallucination, which does not mimic real perception, but is not under voluntary control.
Paraldehyde	Paraldehyde is the cyclic trimer of acetaldehyde molecules. Formally, it is a derivative of 1,3,5-trioxane. The corresponding tetramer is metaldehyde. A colourless liquid, it is sparingly soluble in water and highly soluble in alcohol. Paraldehyde slowly oxidizes in air, turning brown and producing an odor of acetic acid. It quickly reacts with most plastics and rubber.

Chapter 9. TREATMENT

Ketamine	Ketamine is a drug used in human and veterinary medicine. Its hydrochloride salt is sold as Ketanest, Ketaset, and Ketalar. Pharmacologically, ketamine is classified as an NMDA receptor antagonist.
Clonazepam	Clonazepam is a benzodiazepine derivative with anticonvulsant, muscle relaxant, and very potent anxiolytic properties. It is marketed by Roche under the trade-names Klonopin in the United States, and Ravotril in Chile. Other names like Rivotril or Rivatril are known throughout the large majority of the rest of the world. Clonazepam has an unusually long half-life of 18-50 hours, making it generally considered to be among the long-acting benzodiazepines. Clonazepam is a chlorinated derivative of nitrazepam and therefore a nitrobenzodiazepine.
NEUROTRANSMITTER	Neurotransmitters are endogenous chemicals which transmit signals from a neuron to a target ce across a synapse. Neurotransmitters are packaged into synaptic vesicles clustered beneath the membrane on the presynaptic side of a synapse, and are released into the synaptic cleft, where they bind to receptors in the membrane on the postsynaptic side of the synapse. Release of neurotransmitters usually follows arrival of an action potential at the synapse, but may also follov graded electrical potentials.
Designer drug	Designer drug is a term used to describe drugs which are created (or marketed, if they had already existed) to get around existing drug laws, usually by modifying the molecular structures of existing drugs to varying degrees, or less commonly by finding drugs with entirely different chemical structures that produce similar subjective effects to illegal recreational drugs. History United States 1920s-1930s The term "designer drug" was first coined by law enforcement in the 1980s, and has gained widespread use. However the first appearance of what would now be termed designer drugs occurred well before this, in the 1920s.

Chapter 9. TREATMENT

Sibutramine	Sibutramine is an oral anorexiant. Until recently it was marketed and prescribed as an adjunct in the treatment of exogenous obesity along with diet and exercise. It has been associated with increased cardiovascular events and strokes and has been withdrawn from the market in the United States, the UK, the EU, Australia, Canada, Hong Kong, Thailand and Mexico and recently in India following the decision of an expert committee on its effects on CVS (SCOUT report).
Posttraumatic stress disorder	Posttraumatic stress disorder is a severe anxiety disorder that can develop after exposure to any event that results in psychological trauma. This event may involve the threat of death to oneself or to someone else, or to one's own or someone else's physical, sexual, or psychological integrity, overwhelming the individual's ability to cope. As an effect of psychological trauma, Posttraumatic stress disorder is less frequent and more enduring than the more commonly seen acute stress response.
Acetaldehyde	Acetaldehyde is an organic chemical compound with the formula CH_3CHO or MeCHO. It is one of the most important aldehydes, occurring widely in nature and being produced on a large scale industrially. Acetaldehyde occurs naturally in coffee, bread, and ripe fruit, and is produced by plants as part of their normal metabolism. It is also produced by oxidation of ethanol and is popularly believed to be a cause of hangovers. Pathways of exposure include air, water, land or groundwater that can expose the human subject directly if they inhale, drink, or smoke.
Acetylcholine	The chemical compound acetylcholine is a neurotransmitter in both the peripheral nervous system (PNS) and central nervous system (CNS) in many organisms including humans. Acetylcholine is one of many neurotransmitters in the autonomic nervous system (ANS) and the only neurotransmitter used in the motor division of the somatic nervous system. (Sensory neurons use glutamate and various peptides at their synapses). Acetylcholine is also the principal neurotransmitter in all autonomic ganglia.
Beta blocker	Beta blockers are a class of drugs used for various indications, but particularly for the management of cardiac arrhythmias, cardioprotection after myocardial infarction (heart attack), and hypertension. As beta adrenergic receptor antagonists, they diminish the effects of epinephrine (adrenaline) and other stress hormones. In 1958 the first beta blocker, dichloroisoproterenol, was synthesised by Eli Lilly Laboratories, but it was Sir James W. Black in 1962, who found the first clinically significant use of beta blockers with propranolol and pronethalol; it revolutionized the medical management of angina pectoris and is considered by many to be one of the most important contributions to clinical medicine and pharmacology of the 20th century.

Chapter 9. TREATMENT

Butorphanol	Butorphanol is a morphinan-type synthetic opioid analgesic. Brand name Stadol was recently discontinued by the manufacturer. It is now only available in its generic formulations, manufactured by Novex, Mylan, Apotex and Ben Venue Laboratories. Butorphanol is most closely structurally related to levorphanol. Butorphanol is available only as butorphanol tartrate in injectable and intranasal spray formulations.
Tramadol	Tramadol hydrochloride is a centrally acting opioid analgesic, used in treating moderate to severe pain. The drug has a wide range of applications, including treatment for restless leg syndrome and fibromyalgia. It was developed by the pharmaceutical company Grünenthal GmbH in the late 1970s.
Amlodipine	Amlodipine is a long-acting calcium channel blocker (dihydropyridine class) used as an anti-hypertensive and in the treatment of angina. Like other calcium channel blockers, amlodipine acts by relaxing the smooth muscle in the arterial wall, decreasing total peripheral resistance and hence reducing blood pressure; in angina it increases blood flow to the heart muscle.
Ibogaine	Ibogaine is a naturally occurring psychoactive substance found in a number of plants, principally in a member of the Apocynaceae family known as iboga (Tabernanthe iboga). A hallucinogen, the substance is banned in some countries; in other countries it is being used to treat addiction to opiates, methamphetamine and other drugs. Derivatives of ibogaine that lack the substance's hallucinogen properties are under development.
Ketoconazole	Ketoconazole is a synthetic antifungal drug used to prevent and treat skin and fungal infections, especially in immunocompromised patients such as those with AIDS or those on chemotherapy. Ketoconazole is sold commercially as an anti-dandruff shampoo, topical cream, and oral tablet, under the trademark name Nizoral by Johnson ' Johnson in the USA, and as Sebizole by Douglas Pharmaceuticals in Australia ' New Zealand. In Spain products with ketoconazole as main agent include Ketoisdin gel 2% (gel) and Fungarest (topical 30g cream).
Pergolide	Pergolide is an ergoline-based dopamine receptor agonist used in some countries for the treatment of Parkinson's disease.

	Parkinson's disease is associated with low levels of the neurotransmitter dopamine in the brain. Pergolide has some of the same effects as dopamine in the body.
Riluzole	Riluzole is a drug used to treat amyotrophic lateral sclerosis. It delays the onset of ventilator-dependence or tracheostomy in selected patients and may increase survival by approximately 3-5 months. It is marketed by Sanofi-Aventis with the brand name Rilutek.
Tiagabine	Tiagabine is an anti-convulsive medication produced by Cephalon and marketed under the brand name Gabitril. The drug was discovered at Novo Nordisk in Denmark in 1988 and was co-developed with Abbott. After a period of co-promotion, Cephalon licensed Tiagabine from Abbott/Novo and now is the exclusive producer. The medication is also used in the treatment of panic disorder, as are a few other anticonvulsants.
Psychiatric medication	A psychiatric medication is a licensed psychoactive drug taken to exert an effect on the mental state and used to treat mental disorders. Usually prescribed in psychiatric settings, these medications are typically made of synthetic chemical compounds, although some are naturally occurring, or at least naturally derived. Administration Prescription psychiatric medications, like all prescription medications, require a prescription from a physician, such as a psychiatrist, or a psychiatric nurse practitioner, PMHNP, before they can be obtained.
Psychopharmacology	Psychopharmacology is the study of drug-induced changes in mood, sensation, thinking, and behavior.

Chapter 9. TREATMENT

The field of psychopharmacology studies a wide range of substances with various types of psychoactive properties. The professional and commercial fields of pharmacology and psychopharmacology do not mainly focus on psychedelic or recreational drugs, as the majority of studies are conducted for the development, study, and use of drugs for the modification of behavior and the alleviation of symptoms, particularly in the treatment of mental disorders (psychiatric medication).

Tranquilizer

A tranquilizer, is a drug that induces tranquillity in an individual.

The term "tranquilizer" is imprecise, and is usually qualified, or replaced with more precise terms:

- minor tranquilizer usually refers to anxiolytic or antianxiety agent

- major tranquilizer usually refers to antipsychotics

Antimanic agents can also be considered tranquilizing agents.

In music

- "Tranquilizer" is a song written by Tom Stephan ' Neil Tennant, from album Superchumbo "WowieZowie" (2005).

- Tranquilizer by Fat Jon The Ample Soul Physician, from album Repaint Tomorow

Phencyclidine

Phencyclidine (a complex clip of the chemical name 1-(1-phenylcyclohexyl)piperidine, commonly initialized as PCP), also known as angel dust and myriad other street names, is a recreational, dissociative drug formerly used as an anesthetic agent, exhibiting hallucinogenic and neurotoxic effects.

	Developed in 1926, it was first patented in 1952 by the Parke-Davis pharmaceutical company and marketed under the brand name Sernyl. In chemical structure, PCP is an arylcyclohexylamine derivative, and, in pharmacology, it is a member of the family of dissociative anesthetics. PCP works primarily as an NMDA receptor antagonist, which blocks the activity of the NMDA receptor and, like most antiglutamatergic hallucinogens, is significantly more dangerous than other categories of hallucinogens. Other NMDA receptor antagonists include ketamine, tiletamine, and dextromethorphan. Although the primary psychoactive effects of the drug lasts for a few hours, the total elimination rate from the body typically extends eight days or longer.
Fluvoxamine	Fluvoxamine is an antidepressant which functions as a selective serotonin reuptake inhibitor (SSRI). Fluvoxamine was first approved by the U.S. Food and Drug Administration (FDA) in 1993 for the treatment of obsessive compulsive disorder (OCD). Fluvoxamine CR (controlled release) is approved to treat social anxiety disorder. Fluvoxamine is also prescribed to treat major depressive disorder (MDD) and anxiety disorders, such as generalized anxiety disorder (GAD), panic disorder, and post-traumatic stress disorder (PTSD).
Histamine antagonist	A histamine antagonist is an agent that inhibits action of histamine via histamine receptors. H_1 antihistamines are used as treatment for symptoms of allergies, such as runny nose. Allergies are caused by an excessive type 1 hypersensitivity response of the body to allergens, such as pollen released by plants. An allergic reaction, which if severe enough can lead to anaphylaxis, results in excessive release of histamines and other mediators by the body. Other uses of H_1 antihistamines help with symptoms of local inflammation that result from various conditions, such as insect stings, even if there is no allergic reaction. Other commonly used examples of antihistamines include the H_2 antagonists (cimetidine), which are widely used for the treatment of acid reflux and stomach ulcers, as they decrease gastric acid production.
Diphenhydramine	Diphenhydramine hydrochloride is a first generation antihistamine mainly used to treat allergies. Like most other first generation antihistamines, the drug also has a powerful hypnotic effect, and for this reason is often used as a nonprescription sleep aid and a mild anxiolytic. The drug also acts as an antiemetic.
Paliperidone	Paliperidone is an atypical antipsychotic developed by Janssen Pharmaceutica. Invega is an extended release formulation of paliperidone that uses the OROS extended release system to allow for once-daily dosing. Invega Sustenna (paliperidone palmitate) is a long-acting injectable formulation of paliperidone indicated for once-monthly injection after an initial titration period. Chemically, paliperidone is the primary active metabolite of the older atypical antipsychotic risperidone (paliperidone is 9-hydroxyrisperidone, i.e. risperidone with an extra hydroxyl group).

Chapter 9. TREATMENT

Trazodone	Trazodone is an antidepressant of the serotonin antagonist and reuptake inhibitor (SARI) class. It is a phenylpiperazine compound. Trazodone also has anxiolytic, and hypnotic effects. Trazodone has considerably less prominent anticholinergic (dry mouth, constipation, tachycardia) and sexual side effects than most of the tricyclic antidepressants (TCAs).
Cortisol	Cortisol is a steroid hormone, or glucocorticoid, produced by the adrenal gland. It is released in response to stress and a low level of blood glucocorticoids. Its primary functions are to increase blood sugar through gluconeogenesis; suppress the immune system; and aid in fat, protein and carbohydrate metabolism. It also decreases bone formation. Various synthetic forms of cortisol are used to treat a variety of different diseases.
Isocarboxazid	Isocarboxazid is an irreversible and nonselective monoamine oxidase inhibitor (MAOI) of the hydrazine chemical class used as an antidepressant and anxiolytic. It is one of the few hydrazine MAOIs still in clinical use, along with phenelzine.
	Isocarboxazid is used to combat numerous medical problems, such as: depression, social anxiety, panic disorder and also is in the process of becoming a medication to aid in the fight against Parkinson's and other dementia-related disorders.
Psychoactive drug	A psychoactive drug, psychopharmaceutical, or psychotropic is a chemical substance that crosses the blood-brain barrier and acts primarily upon the central nervous system where it affects brain function, resulting in changes in perception, mood, consciousness, cognition, and behavior. These substances may be used recreationally, to purposefully alter one's consciousness, as entheogens, for ritual, spiritual, and/or shamanic purposes, as a tool for studying or augmenting the mind, or therapeutically as medication.
	Because psychoactive substances bring about subjective changes in consciousness and mood that the user may find pleasant (e.g. euphoria) or advantageous (e.g. increased alertness), many psychoactive substances are abused, that is, used excessively, despite the health risks or negative consequences.

Chapter 9. TREATMENT

Tranylcypromine	Tranylcypromine is a drug of the substituted phenethylamine and amphetamine classes which acts as a monoamine oxidase inhibitor (MAOI)--it is a non-selective and irreversible inhibitor of the enzyme monoamine oxidase (MAO). It is used as an antidepressant and anxiolytic agent in the clinical treatment of mood and anxiety disorders, respectively. History Tranylcypromine was originally developed as an analogue of amphetamine.
Anticholinergic	An anticholinergic agent is a substance that blocks the neurotransmitter acetylcholine in the central and the peripheral nervous system. An example of an anticholinergic is dicycloverine, and the classic example is atropine. Anticholinergics are administered to reduce the effects mediated by acetylcholine on acetylcholine receptors in neurons through competitive inhibition. Therefore, their effects are reversible.
Clozapine	Clozapine is an antipsychotic medication used in the treatment of schizophrenia, and is also used off-label in the treatment of bipolar disorder. Wyatt. R and Chew. R (2005) tells us there are three pharmaceutical companies that market this drug at present: Novartis Pharmaceuticals (manufacturer), Mylan Laboratories and Ivax Pharmaceuticals (market generic clozapine). The first of the atypical antipsychotics to be developed, it was first introduced in Europe in 1971, but was voluntarily withdrawn by the manufacturer in 1975 after it was shown to cause agranulocytosis, a condition involving a dangerous decrease in the number of white blood cells, that led to death in some patients.
Fluphenazine	Fluphenazine is a typical antipsychotic drug used for the treatment of psychoses such as schizophrenia and acute manic phases of bipolar disorder. It belongs to the piperazine class of phenothiazines. Its main use is as a long acting injection given once every two or three weeks to people with schizophrenia who suffer frequent relapses of illness. Its side effect profile is similar to haloperidol, namely predominantly dopamine-blocking effects which give rise to akathisia, parkinsonism and tremor. Long term side effects include the potentially irreversible tardive dyskinesia and the potentially fatal neuroleptic malignant syndrome.

Chapter 9. TREATMENT

Molindone	Molindone is a therapeutic antipsychotic, used in the treatment of schizophrenia. It works by blocking the effects of dopamine in the brain, leading to diminished psychoses. It is rapidly absorbed when taken by mouth. It is sometimes described as a typical antipsychotic, and sometimes described as an atypical antipsychotic.
Phenothiazine	Phenothiazine is an organic compound that occurs in various antipsychotic and antihistaminic drugs. It has the formula $S(C_6H_4)_2NH$. This yellow tricyclic compound is soluble in acetic acid, benzene, and ether. The compound is related to the thiazine-class of heterocyclic compounds. Derivatives of the parent compound find wide use as drugs.
Amoxapine	Amoxapine is a tetracyclic antidepressant (TeCA) of the dibenzoxazepine class. Though some authorities classify it as a secondary amine tricyclic antidepressant. Amoxapine is used in the treatment of depression, anxiety disorders, panic disorder, and bipolar disorder.
Clomipramine	Clomipramine is a tricyclic antidepressant (TCA). It was developed in the 1960s by the Swiss drug manufacturer Geigy (now known as Novartis) and has been in clinical use worldwide ever since.

- Obsessive compulsive disorder (OCD) approved by the U.S. Food and Drug Administration (FDA)
- Major depression
- Panic disorder with or without agoraphobia
- Narcolepsy
- Premature ejaculation
- Depersonalization disorder
- Chronic pain with or without organic disease, particular headache of the tension type
- Enuresis (involuntary nightly urinating in sleep) in children and adolescents
- Cataplexy

Clomipramine had been used experimentally to reduce relapses in cocaine addicts, and to repair neurotransmitter damage caused by cocaine; however, further studies are needed in this area.

Chapter 9. TREATMENT

Maprotiline	Maprotiline is a tetracyclic antidepressant (TeCA). It is a strong norepinephrine reuptake inhibitor with only weak effects on serotonin and dopamine reuptake.

It exerts blocking effects at the following postsynaptic receptors:

- Strong : H_1
- Moderate : $5\text{-}HT_2$, $alpha_1$
- Weak : D_2, mACh

The pharmacologic profile of Maprotiline explains its antidepressant, sedative, anxiolytic, and sympathomimetic activities. Additionally, it shows a strong antagonism against Reserpine-induced effects in animal studies, as do the other 'classical' antidepressants. Although Maprotiline behaves in most regards as a 'first generation antidepressant' it is commonly referred to as 'second generation antidepressant'.

Trimipramine

Trimipramine is a tricyclic antidepressant (TCA). It has antidepressant, anxiolytic, antipsychotic, sedative, and analgesic effects.

Indications

- Endogenous and neurotic depression with prominent agitation and anxiety
- Depressive and non-depressive insomnia (suitable for long-term treatment)
- Adjunctive therapy of alcohol and opioid withdrawal
- Chronic pain of malignant and non-malignant origin

Benzatropine

Benzatropine is an anticholinergic marketed under the trade name Cogentin which is used in the treatment of Parkinson's disease, parkinsonism, akathisia, and dystonia.
Benzatropine is used in patients to reduce the side effects of antipsychotic treatment, such as parkinsonism and akathisia. Benzatropine is also a second-line drug for the treatment of Parkinson's disease.

Flurazepam

Flurazepam is a drug which is a benzodiazepine derivative. It possesses anxiolytic, anticonvulsant, sedative and skeletal muscle relaxant properties. It produces a metabolite with a very long half-life (40-250 hours), which may stay in the bloodstream for up to four days.

Chapter 9. TREATMENT

Oxazepam	Oxazepam is a drug which is a benzodiazepine derivative. Oxazepam is a benzodiazepine used extensively since the 1960s for the treatment of anxiety and insomnia and in the control of symptoms of alcohol withdrawal. It is a metabolite of diazepam, prazepam and temazepam. Oxazepam has moderate amnesic, anxiolytic, anticonvulsant, hypnotic, sedative and skeletal muscle relaxant properties compared to other benzodiazepines.
Perphenazine	Perphenazine is a typical antipsychotic drug. Chemically, it is classified as a piperazinyl phenothiazine. It has been in clinical use for decades. Perphenazine is roughly five times as potent as chlorpromazine; thus perphenazine is considered a medium-potency antipsychotic.
Pimozide	Pimozide is an antipsychotic drug of the diphenylbutylpiperidine class. It was discovered at Janssen Pharmaceutica in 1963. It has a high potency compared to chlorpromazine (ratio 50-70:1). On a weight basis it is even more potent than haloperidol. It also has special neurologic indications for Tourette syndrome and resistant tics. The side effects include akathisia, tardive dyskinesia, and, more rarely, neuroleptic malignant syndrome and long QT syndrome.
Pindolol	Pindolol is a nonselective beta blocker with partial beta-adrenergic receptor agonist activity. It possesses ISA (Intrinsic Sympathomimetic Activity). This means that pindolol particularly in high doses exerts effects like epinephrine or isoprenaline (increased pulse rate, increased blood pressure, bronchodilation), but these effects are limited. Pindolol also shows membrane stabilizing effects like quinidine, possibly accounting for its antiarrhythmic effects. It also functions as a 5-HT1A receptor weak partial agonist / antagonist.
Quazepam	Quazepam is a drug which is a benzodiazepine derivative. Quazepam is indicated for the treatment of insomnia including sleep induction and sleep maintenance. Quazepam induces impairment of motor function and has hypnotic and anticonvulsant properties with less overdose potential than other benzodiazepines.
Thiothixene	Thiothixene is a typical antipsychotic drug of the thioxanthene class used in the treatment of psychoses like schizophrenia. It was introduced in 1965 by Pfizer.
Triazolam	Triazolam is a benzodiazepine derivative drug. It possesses pharmacological properties similar to that of other benzodiazepines, but it is generally only used as a sedative to treat severe insomnia. In addition to the hypnotic properties triazolam possesses, amnesic, anxiolytic, sedative, anticonvulsant and muscle relaxant properties are also present. Due to its short half-life, triazolam is not effective for patients that suffer from frequent awakenings or early wakening.
Trifluoperazine	Trifluoperazine is a typical antipsychotic of the phenothiazine chemical class.

The primary indication of trifluoperazine is schizophrenia. Other official indications may vary country by country, but generally it is also indicated for use in agitation and patients with behavioural problems, severe nausea and vomiting as well as severe anxiety. Its use in many parts of the world has declined because of highly frequent and severe early and late tardive dyskinesia, a type of extrapyramidal symptom. The annual development rate of tardive dyskinesia may be as high as 4%.

Meprobamate

Meprobamate is a carbamate derivative which is used as an anxiolytic drug. It was the best-selling minor tranquilizer for a time, but has largely been replaced by the benzodiazepines.

History

Meprobamate was first synthesized by Bernard John Ludwig, PhD, and Frank Milan Berger, MD, at Carter Products in May 1950. Wallace Laboratories, a subsidiary of Carter Products, bought the license and named it Miltown after the borough of Milltown in New Jersey.

CPSIA information can be obtained at www.ICGtesting.com
Printed in the USA
268809BV00001B/37/P